KNOW
YOUR OWN
MIND

—◆—

**An Amazing Revelation
of Your Inner Consciousness**

Harold Sherman

SQUARE
CIRCLES
PUBLISHING

Contents

Preface

WORDS ARE crude vehicles of human concepts and ideas. But in our state of development, words must be used as best they can in an attempt to convey what is often sensed by the soul beyond the powers of ordinary expression.

It is to be hoped that you, the reader, who earnestly seek true knowledge of self, will open not only your mind but your heart to the concepts and ideas herein presented, putting aside preconceived beliefs and prejudices, thus permitting logic and intuition to sit in judgment.

Only in this manner can you escape the bondage of words, and experience the revelation of truth in your consciousness.

To begin to understand The Great Within, in which your soul resides, you must still the outer voice of Argumentation and learn to listen, as you read, to the inner voice of Wisdom, which will say to you again and again, as you awaken deep convictions within you, "This is true . . . this is true!"

Proceed, therefore, with your mind receptive to possibly new concepts. Prepare to act upon those which appeal as Truth. This is the only way to open the door to The Great Within and to keep it open.

Best wishes!

Harold Sherman

ONE

Your Higher Powers
of Perception

UNIVERSAL CONSCIOUSNESS pervades everywhere and everything. There is no thing without consciousness. While we can ordinarily conceive of consciousness existing in objects and beings, it is more difficult to regard the elements, themselves, as possessing consciousness. Not only does it indwell humans and animals, but vegetables, minerals and the four basic elements—earth, air, water and fire, as well. It functions on every level and is expressed through every object and being within the sensory limitations of that object or being at any given time. As evolutionary changes take place, bringing about a more sensitized condition of objects and beings, a greater and greater awareness of consciousness comes to exist within them.

It is today an established fact in physics that all elements come originally from gases. Astronomers, observing the heavens within the range of Palomar's mighty telescope, have photographed incomprehensibly gigantic gaseous clouds which they say are new galaxies of suns and planets in process of creation. To the eye of man, this stellar panorama would appear to be chaotic in nature, without intelligent design or purpose. But Science now knows that both design and purpose are present throughout the vast reaches of space; that universal

1

consciousness is everywhere at work, at all times, and that no place exists where universal consciousness is not.

Consciousness is intelligence in action. Functioning on the subconscious level, it is constantly seeking new ways to express itself in form. Each environment is a challenge to consciousness to create and adapt forms capable of evolving in it. All life is, therefore, experimental, with myriads of species coming into existence and passing out again as consciousness moves on into new forms which leave the record of their existence in the Great Subconscious. A scientist has said that "the only thing permanent in the Universe, is *change*."

As consciousness evolves through form, it tends to individualize. In Man, all lower forms of life on this earth have been concreted. The experiential intelligence gained by consciousness in its expression through lower forms of life, long since discarded, is now a part of the human organism. Man is inheritor of a body form designed by Universal Intelligence for the indwelling of a state of awareness above and beyond that of any other creature on this planet.

There are, undoubtedly, other beings on other planets and in higher dimensions vastly superior to creature man. But there are conceivably no beings in the universe, having self-conscious identity, who hold greater promise for future development and unimagined attainment, not only here, but in the realms above, in the eternity of time to come.

When consciousness becomes conscious of itself, in any form, it takes on identity and senses, from that time on, the voice of God, the Great Intelligence, saying, "I am I" to it. Once this state of awareness has been reached, consciousness has immortalized itself in form and that form becomes its pattern for eternal evolution and expression.

Self-conscious identification with the God Consciousness is the goal of all creation. Every particle of consciousness is constantly seeking its affinity. This affinity is provided so that nothing in nature is without its balancing counterpart. There is a positive and negative charge in all things. The Universe, itself, is electromagnetic. Behind each electrical impulse is thought and behind thought is the God Consciousness from whence thought originates. God then, through His electromagnetic circuit, is able to keep in constant communication with each particle and form and identity in His expanding creation, although much of it is still unconscious of Him and its origin in Him. This is because many elements of creation have not yet evolved to self-conscious levels and because God, the Great Intelligence, maintains absolute *impersonality* in relation to all parts of His creation, high or low.

There is a profound justice in such impersonality since it guarantees the exercise of free will for those beings attaining an awareness of the God Presence within them, and grants them the choice of personalizing God in their lives and consciousness by approaching closer and closer to Him in thought and feeling through higher and higher mental and spiritual development.

Primitive man conceived of God as a mighty Being, seated on a throne in the heavens, meting out the most horrendous punishment to sinning mortals. They felt that God was spying on their every thought and act, and were constrained to obey their interpretation of His laws through fear rather than love.

It is true that every thought and deed we have committed is recorded in consciousness and continues to exist but God, as a Being, will not read these records. However, God's unchangeable laws are such that we can never escape the ultimate penalty of our own violation of these laws in any plane of our being—physical, mental, emotional or spiritual. We may think, for a time, that we have outwitted or eluded possible retribution in some form, for an unwise, dishonest or destructive thought or act, but so infallible is the functioning of the universal laws of cause and effect, they will most certainly exact their payment in kind, in due course. This is what is meant by the term so often used and so little understood—*eternal justice*. All life is governed by these laws which rule planets as well as men.

Once consciousness evolves to a self-conscious level in any form, such as man, the resultant identity must thereafter assume personal responsibility for his thoughts and acts. He is now, in a very real sense, a son of God in the making and, having become aware of the Father, whatever his concept of God in the beginning, he has made sufficient attunement to be held individually accountable by the laws governing his being.

When Man became conscious of a power greater than himself, a sense of personal accountability was born and Conscience came into existence. Since God is fundamentally Good, Man cannot be fundamentally bad. But Man, as a free will creature and creator, within certain limitations, of his own destiny, can so misuse and pervert his God-given creative powers that he can create evil and eventually destroy himself, with consequent loss of identity and return to the Great Subconscious.

Today, as in all past times, God has not intervened to keep Man from warring against his fellow man. The God Consciousness never functions in this manner. All prayers for peace by the unchanged of heart, however well-intentioned, cannot and will never bring peace. If all or most men reached such a state of development that they became conscious of the God Presence within them, peace would instantly come to the world. But it is Man's job, not God's—to solve the problems of his own making here. He possesses, within his consciousness, all of the power and resources necessary to create a heaven on earth, if he so chooses. It has taken Man centuries to learn this one simple fact—and he has still not learned it.

He still chooses to achieve what he feels is right by force. He places reliance upon material weapons and powers. He fills his mind with fears and hates and prejudices and doubts and suspicions, keeping himself under constant tension and turmoil. His religions support him in his attitudes. He professes to believe in his concept of God and calls upon God to help him destroy his enemies. He is, for the most part, totally unacquainted with the God Presence in his consciousness, for he reflects little or none of it in his life. This is the picture of Man on earth today, who is one step away from self-annihilation, when one step in the opposite direction, toward the God Consciousness within, could cast a great new light of hope over this small, dark planet.

Never before, in all earth history, has Man stood at such a crossroads. By awakening to a realization of the God Power within him, he can lift himself and all humanity with him, to a new level of consciousness which will awaken new senses for his better perception of the universe about him, and for a better understanding of his fellow humans. Man can never cope with the Great Without until he has learned to draw guidance, wisdom and protection from the Great Within.

It is already half past eleven. In the half hour of relative time that Man has left, he must find himself in the God Consciousness.

World consciousness is, of course, Man's consciousness multiplied by every human being now existent on this planet. The dominant thought in this world consciousness at any given moment or period of time determines the conditions in the world. Identified with this current world consciousness is the vibratory influence of all past thoughts and feelings generated by human creatures in all past times. Since like attracts like, a war-like attitude on the part of millions of humans becomes attuned to similar thought forms still contained within the mental ether envelope which surrounds this earth. This partially explains why history seems to repeat itself with recurring cycles of wars and rumors of wars which are simply the externalization, at times, of mass thought.

What you, as an individual, think and feel is making its constructive or destructive contribution to the thought content of the world in which you live. Since what is in consciousness always seeks outer expression, the human race will never rise above wars and warring until it raises the level of its consciousness to the point that no future strife is possible.

Your physical body is the most sensitized instrument on earth. It may not function with the mechanical precision of a man-made machine, which automatically repeats a process, for your body is subject to growth and change and it has not even begun to approach its maximum of refinement and sensitivity. There is a constant interplay of forces within your physical organism from the moment it is conceived and your consciousness takes possession of it.

Its five physical senses are the channels through which your consciousness puts out "feelers" in an attempt to interpret what is happening in and about you. How you interpret what your mind senses through sight, hearing, taste, touch and smell, and how you react emotionally to these interpretations determines, to a great degree, your attitude toward life and your capacity to face life.

Up to recent times, few humans have learned to rely upon any higher sensory faculties within them. If they, unexplainably, became aware of some event and condition without the aid of any or all of their five physical senses, they usually attributed this occurrence to a happenstance and gave it little or no conscious reflection.

So prejudicial has been the general public attitude, so dictated by materialistic scientists and orthodox religionists, few humans have dared confess illuminating experiences in consciousness to even their close relatives or friends.

For this reason, scant attention or encouragement has been given by many to the possible development in them of an extended awareness in consciousness. And yet, the very fact that the persistent, spasmodic recurrence of what has long been termed "psychic phenomena" has taken place, time and again, in the lives of men and women of all ages and types and classes, provides undeniable evidence of the existence of these higher powers. Unhappily, a set mind creates its own mold and cannot move out of it unless shattered by an inner or outer experience of such power that the established pattern of thinking is broken.

Today, the external pressures on the consciousness of each human are becoming so great that he must, eventually, look within himself in search of some new strength or new wisdom to meet the soul-testing challenge of everyday living. What is bad for the world can thus become good for the individual human if it can awaken in him the realization of the poverty of his own thinking and the sad and tragic fact that this failure to develop and utilize his God-given higher powers of mind is responsible for the desperately confused conditions which exist on earth.

If the history of the human race were to be written by a higher being possessing the discernment to evaluate Man, at this point, it might contain this statement:

> "This planet has been peopled with amazing little creatures almost totally blind to the existence within them of a God Consciousness. Thus far, these creatures have sought to function with their own limited consciousness and the awareness provided by their extremely restricted physical senses. The progress they have attained has been at unspeakable cost in blood and sacrifice and suffering. Many times these creatures have drawn upon the God Power without realizing it and have advanced because of it.

"But, today, these creatures have reached the limit of their material achievements without acceptance of the God Consciousness and its directing influence in their lives. They have reached the point where their own intelligence is not sufficient, in itself, to cope with the world they have created and the forces they have unleashed in it. They need, now, the wisdom which only their undeveloped and, as yet, largely unrecognized higher perceptions can bring to them."

Viewed impersonally, it will be of interest to see whether or not this experimental life form can or will let the indwelling God Consciousness work through it. If this creature solves his present self-created crisis in this manner, it can be foreseen that he will then emerge into a new state of awareness which will lead him into a new world and liberate him forever from the unbridled urges of the animal nature within him.

It is, of course, profoundly difficult for Man to see himself as he really is or could be, in true perspective. Few humans can assume an attitude of objective impersonality with respect to themselves, and they are so prejudiced in their own thinking that they are just as incapable of accurately appraising anyone else. Conflicting issues in consciousness of race and color and creed and temperament so becloud Man's judgment that he is unable to think freely or clearly upon problems confronting the human race as a whole. Because of this, his tendency is to attempt to force upon his fellow man what he feels would be good for him whether or not these measures are acceptable to those upon whom they would be imposed.

Such attitudes and actions only set up new resistances in human consciousness and drive Man further and further away from any possibility of genuine brotherhood and understanding. As a result, the reservoir of world consciousness seethes with repressed hates and fears and resentments and lust for power and revenge, all of which must boil inevitably to the surface and externalize themselves in some cataclysmic release of human feelings unless this pent-up atomic disturbance in mass consciousness is spiritualized by a basic change in consciousness of the leaders of Mankind. Realistically, if this is too much to hope, then there is little or no hope for the future of humanity on this planet.

You need to know—everyone needs to know—that your physical instrument is actually a highly sensitized receiver and transmitter of thought. Were this one great fact thoroughly recognized by all humans, it would startle them into the exercise of profound caution. Aware that their thoughts expressed in the form of fears and worries have an effect not only upon themselves but upon those nearest and dearest to them, they would seek to gain better emotional and thought control. Aware also, that it was possible for them to tune in on the wrong thinking of others, if their own thoughts were of a like nature, they would strive to elevate their thinking to lift them vibrationally above such destructive mental influences.

Normally, if Man is reasonably well-balanced physically, emotionally and mentally, he is insulated in consciousness, except in unusually disturbed and intensified moments, from the reception of thought impulses from the minds of others, known and unknown. But since the mental ether is filled with emotionally charged thought forms seeking their affinity in the minds of one or more humans, it is not to be wondered at that many men and women are tuning in and out of varying thought conditions in accordance with the nature and quality of their own thinking, at different moments each day and night.

Since consciousness is within and without all things and beings, it presses in upon every developed point of awareness like waters of the sea attempting to seep into every opening and crevice. You exist, in fact, in what might be termed a vast sea of consciousness, much of which is forever subconscious to you. But, in unguarded moments, some of this sea seeps into your own consciousness in the form of stray mental vagaries, impulses and ideas, often so foreign to your own nature as to cause you shock and wonderment at their fleeting existence within you.

You should realize that no thought ever dies. It may change its form through fusion with other thoughts of like character but it exists after emanation from your consciousness and continues an entitized existence of its own on the basis of what it is as created by you. This is, the reason that an individual who has developed his extra sensory faculties can tune in and let himself be influenced by these thought forms which revolve in the mental ether about you or anything which has been connected with you. By interpreting the effect of these thought forms upon him, such a sensitized individual can see in his mind's eye, or feel, the events and conditions of which these thought forms were once a part.

A troubled mind cannot find God—only more trouble. Your consciousness must be cleared of disturbances before it can attract a new and better condition to you. Everything that has come to you in this external life has come as a direct or indirect result of your thinking. You have attracted or repelled different experiences by positive or negative attitudes of mind.

It is impossible to think a thought without launching It upon the electromagnetic ocean of consciousness. Each thought, inherently and inevitably seeks an externalization of itself. If you visualize a certain attainment involving other people, you create the thought form of this achievement which then commences to attract magnetically, in ways incomprehensible to you, the resources and circumstances necessary to the materialization of what you have visualized in actual physical form and fact. If you change any feature or detail of your objective in mind, you automatically set in motion altered thought forms which ultimately bring about like changes in your finally realized attainment.

Because there must be a "meeting of the minds," like again attracting like, where two or more persons are involved in any association or enterprise, a modification of thoughts and desires usually takes place so that the objective accomplished becomes the composite product of all minds engaged therein. Thought is at work in and behind every activity in the universe, however seemingly important or insignificant any activity may appear to be. Thought precedes every action of every form of life, every element, every particle in the cosmos.

It can be seen from this that we, as humans, have made, as yet, very little constructive use of thought. It is seldom that we have entertained thoughts of high inspiration and purpose. It is only infrequently that our thoughts have risen above the level of self interest and selfish desires. The consciousness that is you is made up of the thoughts which you have had concerning everything that has happened to you. You have become aware of only that which you have experienced. The greater awareness which you might have developed in recognition and exercise of your higher powers of perception lies largely still dormant within you. It is this awareness which you and all members of the human race now need to enable you to see in the future something other than a tragic repetition of the past.

Your five physical senses can report only what has happened or will happen again since they are restricted solely to contact with the world outside yourself. But these higher senses were designed to help you see and apprehend and create new worlds not only here but hereafter as the consciousness that is you continues its evolutionary journey through time and space, seeking some day, somewhere, a self-conscious union with the God Consciousness.

To begin, now, to discover and develop your powers of higher perception should be your most consuming desire. Your future happiness, your security, even your life may substantially depend upon what you do with your mind in the next few years to come. Giving thought to the extension of your awareness does not mean the development of telepathic powers, for instance, which may enable you to give parlor demonstrations to your friends. Even if you should find that you were capable of giving such a demonstration in time to come, it would serve little constructive purpose. Any honest failures on your part would be open to ridicule of skeptical, unsympathetic individuals which could easily have such a repercussion upon your consciousness as to impair your own sensitivity and inhibit it from serving you, quietly and effectively, for the protection and guidance of yourself and loved ones.

Those humans who have developed to a high degree these extra sensory faculties hold a deep regard and respect for them and refuse the temptation to use these powers in a frivolous or even commercial manner. A number have been willing to put these powers under test of scientific observers and to exercise them in cases of great human need when some extra sensory knowledge of an individual, a locality or a condition was urgently required. But many of the so-called sensitives, aware of the world's scoffing attitude toward possession of such faculties, withhold a knowledge of their possession from many of their closest friends and relatives. This attitude will probably prevail, for the most part, with a few exceptions, until wider acceptance of these higher sensory powers is shown by science, religion and the public.

When and if you decide to give attention to the development of your own higher powers of consciousness, you should be prepared to put forth a sustained, earnest effort. Your mind will react to your exercise of it like a muscle of your body. Flex your arms fifteen minutes a day, morning and evening, and you will have appreciably larger biceps within a few months' time. The same period of time devoted to the stimulation of your extra sensory perceptive faculties will produce commensurate results.

If at first doubtful that these powers exist, you must accept on faith that they really do. Otherwise, mystics and sensitives and experimenters the world over unanimously testify that these higher powers will not manifest. There is something about their operation which always demands confidence and faith. The mind, in a receptive state, is so suggestible that it will give no evidence of the existence of its higher powers if the individual is strongly skeptical and does not expect results.

It is a waste of time and effort to attempt to demonstrate these powers without any real feeling of conviction or inner urge so to do.

The God Consciousness does not compel you to make attunement with it. Nor are you under any compulsion at any time to learn to make use of extra sensory faculties. But they are there for you whenever you to activate them and they will reward your exercise of them by eventually bringing to you a conscious awareness of your relationship to the God Power within, and your ability to draw upon it for the help and guidance you have long needed but which you have denied yourself by dependence upon the testimony of your five physical senses alone.

You are on the threshold of a new and finer enfoldment of your own real self from the moment you decide to call upon your higher powers of perception to serve you in your daily life.

TWO

Awakening
of Awareness

U NTOLD NUMBERS of humans, living and departed in this
life, have experienced a sudden awareness or a flashing illu-
mination in their interior consciousness which has given them an accurate knowledge of some event, condition or person—past, present
or future—completely beyond the sensory capacity of the five physical
senses. This has had to happen only once in their entire life-time to convince them, beyond any possibility of doubt, that some higher power of
consciousness had operated in and through them. Most of them have
been totally unable to explain the phenomenon except to testify to its
occurrence and to offer the further substantiation of friends or relatives
who were in position to confirm the extra sensory happening.

In some instances, these men and women, due to fixed religious
convictions which have interpreted such developments as the work of
evil forces, have lived in fear of a recurrence of such experiences and
have sought every way to avoid a repetition. In other instances, the
opposite reaction has taken place. Those confronted with the proof of
the existence of these higher powers have either altered, expanded or
renounced their former religious beliefs in order to square them with
their new resultant concepts.

Many authentic cases might be cited, some of which have been reported by world renowned scientists and investigators who have been convinced of the genuineness of extra sensory phenomena. But such cases, already recorded in other books and literature, available to all who wish to make a serious study in this field, serve no purpose by reproduction here. It is more important to emphasize that it is not necessary to refer again and again to time-honored case histories as though the entire proof of extra sensory powers depended largely upon their acceptance, but to show, instead, that such well established evidences of phenomena are only the smallest part of those which have occurred and are occurring.

What happens to you in the way of an extra sensory experience means vastly more than anything that has happened or can happen to anyone else. But you should be most interested in knowing that what could happen to you, at any time, *does* happen to average normal humans like yourself. The testimony of a few of these men and women who have discovered themselves to possess, on occasion, a super sensitive awareness, should serve to convince you, if any convincing is needed, of the potential existence of such powers within your own consciousness.

There has recently been placed in my possession a privately published document entitled, "Reminiscences and Memories of Henry Thomas Butterworth," bearing the publication date of 1886 and containing the fly-leaf statement, "Prepared and left for the information, satisfaction and benefit of my grandchildren and others."

This yellow-leafed booklet was given to me by Frank Butterworth, a great grandson, with the comment that he did not pretend to understand much of its contents but that all members of the Butterworth family were agreed that his great grandfather had been a most remarkable man, an individual of absolute veracity and integrity.

Upon examination of this little volume, I found it to be mainly the account of extra sensory phenomena which Henry Thomas Butterworth had experienced throughout his life. Because his adventures in the realm of mind are so characteristic and representative of the sensitized awareness which has been and is being realized by thousands of men and women, I am letting Mr. Butterworth tell his story to you in his own words:

"This is March 26, 1886, and I am trying to begin and write out as well as I can an account of what some would call my spiritual seeings, feelings and some other experiences from my childhood up, or, as some have called it, my aberrations of mind, my insanities, my imbecilities, etc. This much I will say for myself, viz.: If I ever was insane, aberrant of mind or an imbecile, I have not yet fairly made the discovery, only as a few wiseacres have discovered that there was something rather curious and uncommon about me that astonished them, and that I myself could never tell how it came to be and just why it was, and that sometimes I was as much a wonder to myself than to anybody else, there being a number of instances of something so unlooked for and remarkable that I have been at times deeply impressed that I ought to leave it in writing as well as I could, so that my children and grandchildren and others that it might interest, might, from my experience, get some little insight into some matters that might be of help to them.

"It is not desired that any one should make any use of anything that I shall relate without its actually becoming a benefit to and for them; such experiences frequently becoming guides and helps to an inexperienced one seeking after light and knowledge. . . .

"I am now seventy-seven years of age but my first interior impressions came to me when I was a boy. I had been to school enough to be able to read and pretty well understand common plain English, and write so that it might be read, and no more. I thirsted for knowledge but I was utterly isolated in this thinly settled Ohio country, parents and oldish persons my only associates.

"Was I alone? By no means. I seemed to commune with something invisible—was never lonesome. I have walked between my plow handles hours and days and communed with my precious friends (or intelligences) above. Deep and profound questions would be, with the most perfect distinctness and plainness presented to my mind, as if I myself was the questioner, and then, after a little space of quietude and stillness, would an answer come, most gratifying and satisfactory. . . .

"About 1833, when I was twenty-four years old and married, I, with six others, started to go West to explore new countries. We got to the Wabash River and crossed over seventeen miles, through an unbroken wilderness, to a pioneer's house on the Eel River. On passing from the Wabash to the Eel, a very harassing feeling took possession of me as to home. All was well when I left except our little boy, thirteen months old, was cutting teeth. We were over two hundred miles from home and in a dense forest. I said to my company that if I could not get to feeling better, I should have to leave them and go home. We went down the Eel for one and a half days and got to Loganport at noon. Then and there I left them and pushed for home as fast as I could. I felt nothing different until within a mile of home. I then felt unmistakably that our little boy, Benjamin, had died, was gone. Upon getting home my sister met me in the yard and had the sorrowful news to tell me that our little boy was dead. I told her I knew it already . . .

"Again, not very long after the foregoing, my mother had taken of a poor woman a little daughter of five or six years old to raise. She could do little things. It was short winter days. I had gone twenty or more miles away with a man to look at some land that he wished to sell. About ten o'clock, my friends on the other side of the Styx gave me to understand that I must stop this and go home. I told my friend of my feeling to go home. He insisted on my staying and seeing it more. I did so till noon, when I came to feel so unhappy that I told him I could not and would not stay another moment, and for home I went as fast as my horse could stand it to go.

"I got in sight of the house at dusk; I saw lights moving about; I was more uneasy. There was nobody left at home but my wife, my mother, this little girl and our little children. I had cut and left plenty of wood to serve till I should return. There were some large logs laying in the wood-yard on a descent, and spaces between them. I had put sticks of wood up endways below these to keep them from rolling down. In the evening, this little girl went to get some wood. She took up one of these and turned to go. The log started and struck her down on her face and rolled on till it stopped across her back and shoulders. She being missed, the women began to look for her, and found her in this fix quite dead. It took the help of a neighbor to get the log off her. She had been gotten into the house sometime before I got home. . . .

"Once, in an elevated state of consciousness, seemingly outside my body, I appeared able to look at the inhabitants of earth and see what was the real need and legitimacy of their works and pursuits as they were carrying it on in general, and what proportion was in pursuit of what was about right and necessary. I looked but with a mingled feeling of pity and disgust. Go with your cane to a large ant-hill, thrust it in and stir it up all over and you have an exhibit nearest the real condition and doing of man on earth of anything I can think of, pell-mell, helter skelter, like something crazy, without any real need or use, jolting and tumbling one another around, quarrelling and fighting often, with perhaps one in a hundred going gently and smoothly along, doing about what was needful and best at the time, no more nor less. . . .

At another time, I was given to see that our advances in what we call inventions and improvements had but just begun—just come to the break of day— telegraphy, the telephone and electric light, new or unknown. . . .

"At times, when I have been as if entranced, my inner hearing has caught and taken in that I could call no other than the music of the universe; nothing that I ever met with or heard seemed so melodious and enchanting .

"In these exalted states, I have often returned to earth consciousness with the memory of what I have seen and heard and felt, and I have been left with the impression, time and again, that in all I was made most sensibly to feel and see, I was still only seeing the tip edge of that inconceivable extent of beauty, grandeur, glory and excellence that is before us . . .

"Sometime along here, my thought was turned to our daughter, Ann, who was sixteen or seventeen years of age. This was many years before she was married. I saw her away in the distant future and far away from any friendly aid or help, with several small children, working hard, almost slavishly, to get and give herself and them a subsistence. I told her and her mother both of it at the time; I reminded them both of it in 1880. They remembered it.

"In the interim this had all happened. My daughter had a husband who turned out drunken, lazy and worthless. He disappeared after running through most of what she had. We didn't know where she was for a long time, except to the best of our knowledge she was somewhere in the neighborhood of Pueblo, Colorado, with her little ones, in just the fix I had seen her, years before. She was ashamed to let us know and to ask for the help which we would have been glad to furnish, had we known where to find her. . . .

"There is more yet that wants a place and should be said for the better information and instruction of my grandchildren and great-grandchildren and others. First, idleness, inattention and neglect, meddling with other people's business and affairs and not minding your own business, is a heinous crime, yes, an unpardonable one. It is mean and low not to be employed, and that at and in something that is thoroughly for good and for use for yourself or for your fellow mortals. Idleness, inattention and neglect are the bane of your physical and spiritual life, happiness and existence.

"Be industrious, minding your own business and duties, and let other people mind theirs; let your preaching in the main be a good example. If you go to a neighbor on an errand, name at once your business, fix and do whatever is to be done in the case and get out of his way immediately; don't allow yourself to be an interruption to him, his business or to persons in his employ."

These last commentaries of Mr. Butterworth obviously have nothing to do with the higher powers of mind but they do serve to convey an idea of the principles of the man and the directness of his character. His accounts of his experiences have the ring of authenticity to them in the light of what we have now come to know about the functioning of extra sensory perceptive faculties. These impressions came to Mr. Butterworth unsought. As he testifies, he became conscious of this awareness when a small boy and, by giving attention to it, caused it to develop and serve him with benefit many times during his life. What he did, countless other men and women have quietly done, taking care not to confess their sensitivity to anyone but their most trusted friends and loved ones, for fear they would be misunderstood.

Recently, while lecturing in Cincinnati, I met William Holtz, retired Wire Chief for the Western Union Telegraph Company, who gave me the following well confirmed report of a precognitive experience which had, come to him in the year 1905.

He said: "My tour of duty in those days occupied the hours between 5:45 P.M. and 1:15 A.M. I was the Assistant Night Wire Chief.

Early that year, on one of the heavy routes of Western Union in the northern part of Ohio where our lines paralleled the high tension lines for some distance, there had been a great storm and our wires had become crossed which caused considerable damage, such as blown out fuses, buckled ground plates on switchboards and other destruction at various test stations along the way. This trouble had occurred during the day hours and several months prior to the experience which I am about to relate.

"The Late Night Wire Chief comes on duty each night at 12:30 A.M. and works until 8 A.M. Due to an illness which developed in a member of his family, he requested a leave of absence for one week and I was appointed to take his place.

"The moment I was asked to relieve him, my mind was suddenly filled with the apprehension that, my first night on the job, there would occur a repetition of what had happened some months before in this other section of Ohio. I saw the whole event take place in that instant, in my mind, and I saw myself working frantically, pulling switches and doing everything I could to try and avert as much damage as possible. The impression was so strong and so indelibly pictured in my mind that I couldn't sleep for thinking about it. There were a few days remaining before I was to go on this relief assignment but I finally couldn't stand it any longer. I decided to tell the night chief operator and the late night wire chief of this inexplicable feeling.

"They both laughed at me and suggested that I was taking my coming responsibility too seriously, declaring that what had happened a few months ago would probably never happen again. The word got around the station that I had predicted I was going to have a bad night my first night on duty and I had to take a lot of kidding about it. But, despite everything, this impression grew more and more certain as I approached the night for my tour of duty and I could even see in my mind that this trouble was going to break loose between 2:30 A.M. and the hour when I would be relieved.

"Sure enough—it happened just as I had pictured! At 2:40 A.M., I couldn't believe my eyes when signals on the switchboard indicated what was taking place. There was no time to lose. We worked fast, scarcely knowing where our energy or ability came from. Much damage resulted from the breaking of the high tension line which fell across the Western Union lead.

"When it was all over, those whom I had tried to warn against this happening and who had been so amused at my apprehension, now gathered around to ask how I had known, to the point of insisting, that this would take place. I told them I couldn't explain it; that the picture just occupied my mind and I simply couldn't shake it off. I have never in my life had anything take hold of my mind like that did. It had worried me sick but, strangely enough, just as soon as this incident was over, my mind was as free as though nothing had ever happened."

This was the only extra sensory experience of Mr. Holtz' life but one which left a lasting impression upon him as it did upon all who shared the experience with him.

William Futterman, Chicago advertising man, told me, personally, of an unforgettable incident in his own life when he was a child of five. His mother was dead and he was visiting a cousin's family in the country. At night he had need to go to the outdoor toilet some distance from the house. The older cousin took him out, pushed him inside, then ran back to the house and shut the door, leaving the little fellow terrified and alone. He cried out, instinctively, for his mother, and she appeared out of the darkness, took his hand, spoke comfortingly to him, led him back through the blackness of the night and placed his hand on the door knob. As he opened the door, she disappeared.

Mr. Futterman said, "I can't understand it but I saw my mother plainly and felt my hand in hers. I heard her speak. I still remember this incident as one of the most real experiences of my life."

My father's cousin, Harvey A. Sherman, a Thirty-Third Degree Mason and official stenographer for the 36th Judicial Circuit Court at Cassopolis, Michigan for over fifty years, sent me two carefully written accounts of extra sensory experiences shortly before his demise. He said that, while they were extremely personal, he wished me to have them on record for study and for whatever value they might serve in an investigation of these phenomena.

He confided that, since a young man, he had discovered that he could go to bed and could suggest to himself that he would like to visit his old home town of Traverse City, Michigan, or some other former place of sentimental interest, and that he would proceed to dream of being at that location when he fell asleep. He stated that his dreams were so vivid, they could hardly be distinguished from a waking experience.

"There was one dream that I had again and again," Harvey wrote. "I used to swim in the old Boardman River, and I would always go with the boys, in the old days, along the river bank and cross the dam at the Company's Grist Mill. I was a grown man and had been away from the town for quite some years when I would feel myself, in this dream, going down the river bank until I came to a bridge. I would go down under the north end of it, climb through the scaffolding underneath the bridge, and try to cross on a plank extending from the bank of the stream out to the first pier in the water. A little beyond the pier, the plank ended. At this point, I always awakened, disturbed and disappointed. I could not remember that bridge having been there when I lived in Traverse City, nor the scaffolding, nor the plank. Everything else in the scene had been familiar.

"Finally, the opportunity came to return to the old home town for a visit with your father. I arrived on the evening train but the first thing in the morning, as I was walking downtown to the store with your father, I asked him to go around and along the river bank. In reply to his inquiry as to the reason, I told him I wanted to get something out of my mind.

"Upon reaching the top of a little sandy hill, I stopped in amazement and exclaimed: 'There it is!' In explaining to your father the facts of my dream, he doubted my story, thinking I had seen the bridge before. However, he knew I had not been in Traverse City for years and when I told him of the conditions which I felt existed under the north end of the bridge which we could not see from where we stood, it was agreed that we would investigate. I said that, if my impressions were right, we would find the old scaffolding and the plank, ending beyond the abutment. They were there, just as I had seen them and described them to him!

"I never dreamed of the bridge again but, after the many experiences I have had in this dream state, I firmly believe that we can leave our bodies—that our spirits, driven by a sufficiently strong motive, can take us many miles from our place of residence."

The second demonstration of extra sensory phenomena which Harvey Sherman reported had occurred in his wife Ada's family, some years before. The account is as follows:

"The husband of Ada's aunt died, leaving two small children for her to care for and, as far as she knew, very little money, following payment of sick and funeral expenses. After the lapse of a few days, the mother of the widow confided to her daughter that her son-in-law had visited her three nights in succession, telling her to tell 'Ollie,' the widow, to go to the bank in Cassopolis. The interviews were so real that the mother always maintained that she saw and talked with her son-in-law and asked him to go away and not bother her. But he told her that he would continue to come until she had Ollie get the money in the bank.

"The two women were so disturbed over the incident that they told Ada's father about it. He, being a doctor, took nothing for granted but brought his sister-in-law the six miles from Vandalia to the bank at Cassopolis. They found on deposit in the Cassopolis bank more than three thousand dollars to the credit of Ada's uncle. With this money, the widow was able to go into the millinery business and was enabled to give her two children a good education and fine support."

I am indebted to Alfred Putnam Goodell of Salem, Massachusetts, for this report of an extra sensory experience which is vouched for by his wife. He writes:

"My mother died unexpectedly around one in the morning. My wife and I went to bed tired out from watching and helping her during the day and left my aunt Lizzie sitting up by her bedside. The doctor had assured us that mother would remain with us for at least a week longer, so when we went to bed we had no thought in our minds of her passing away, and were in deep sleep when, suddenly, I awaked and sat up in bed, not knowing what had struck me.

"There, floating over my head and across my face, was my mother, smiling and dressed in her usual garments, and waving her hand, she passed apparently out of the window, but really, I suppose, into her future environment. I awakened my wife by jumping up so suddenly in bed and, under my breath, I said to her: 'See! Look! Mother is there—passing over us and away! She is dead. Let's go down and find out.'

"My wife did not see the vision and laughed at me, but in just a few minutes, Aunt Lizzie came slowly creeping up the stairs and, quietly opening our bedroom door, whispered, 'Are you awake?', to which we both replied, `Yes, come in!' and, with tears streaming down her face, she told us that mother had just died in her arms.

"Now I am not a mystic or a spiritualist, and I never took much stock in spirits, materializations, etc., but you never will be able to shut out that wonderful, vivid disclosure of a soul passing from the body as mother left this realm. I have studied about this experience many, many times, and I have come to the conclusion that mother assumed worldly garb only to acquaint me as to who she was and to assure me she was now through suffering and on her way happily to meet above or wherever our departed go."

John M. Burton of Albuquerque, New Mexico, has written me the account of a harrowing extra sensory experience which occurred to him in December, 1947:

"I think I should assure you at the outset that I do not drink nor take any drugs and that I was in normal health and spirits when this weird happening took place. I was travelling alone from Gloversville, New York, to New York City, and interrupted my journey by car to spend the night at a hotel in Hudson, New York. For reasons which will appear obvious, I will not give the name of the hotel.

"I was assigned a room on the third floor and the floor seemed to be deserted, with no sounds or signs of other guests. I went for a walk about the city in the early evening and, upon returning to my room, decided to do some work on some books of account of a partnership in which I was interested. Before starting this work, I went out to the wash room. While walking to it, while in it, and while walking back to my room, I was oppressed by a growing feeling of loneliness such as I had never before known. This increased and was really uncomfortable.

"However, I sat down at the table in my room and commenced work. The lonely feeling persisted and gradually changed into something else. This other feeling grew stronger and stronger, a feeling I had never previously experienced, nor have I since. The feeling was just this: I felt as if there were a very powerful, invisible presence in that room that was malevolent and extremely evil, with no redeeming, kind qualities whatever. This presence, in back of me, was inaudibly ordering me to get out of that room right away, most emphatically and in an intensely hostile manner. The feeling steadily grew in intensity.

"I felt that this must be a product of my imagination and decided to put it out of my mind and do my work but I could not. It became too strong to be ignored. I debated with myself whether to resist this feeling and prove myself stronger than it, whatever its nature, or whether to get up and get out of there.

"Well, I held out for a few minutes but it was so powerful and so horrible and so very malevolent that I could not take it. I thought that if I stayed there overnight, I might become crazy.

"So, resisting a feeling of haste, since I felt that I was observed, I packed my suitcase with as much dignity as I could muster, and left the room. I went downstairs to the hotel desk and informed the clerk (it was then 11 P.M.) that I had found that business called me elsewhere but that I would pay for the room.

"The clerk insisted that I did not need to pay for the room and he said these exact words: 'I am going to have that room stripped in the morning.'

"I went out of the door calmly enough, wondering if that being, or whatever it was, would keep with me. I crossed to the parking lot and started my car. As I drove away, I found that the feeling had left me completely and I felt at peace. I went on perhaps fifteen or twenty miles and stopped for the night at a small country hotel. I slept peacefully and the mental atmosphere in that room was serene and untroubled in great contrast to that of the first room.

"In trying to figure out why I had felt as I did, I wondered first if there was actually a presence in that room or if there was some sort of electrical apparatus in the neighborhood that was setting up vibrations of very high frequency, or if some local experimenter had been trying to see if some apparatus he had made would produce strange effects upon people. The clerk's remark also made me wonder just why he had spoken as he did. He hadn't seemed surprised at my giving up the room.

"A few weeks later, I related this experience to a cousin of mine and was shocked when he informed me that he had read in a newspaper, shortly before my stay, that an escaped lunatic had murdered a guest in that very hotel."

A study is now being made by Dr. J. B. Rhine and other parapsychologists, of the existence of extra sensory perception in animals. We know so very little, as yet, about the activity of consciousness in any life forms, but this is an experience to which I can personally attest since I knew the principals involved.

Billy Connors was one of the outstanding showmen of Indiana. He was an energetic little man who possessed a huge Great Dane dog. When I called on Billy and his wife, Torchy, at their home in Marion a few years ago, I was met at the door by the Great Dane, and almost bowled over. She was a magnificent animal and demonstrated an unusual attachment for Billy, responding to his every command. The two were inseparable. Wherever Billy went, the Great Dane went. And so, some time later, when Billy's health failed and he was compelled to seek a different climate, he and Torchy and the Great Dane moved to Pueblo, Colorado.

In February of 1952, Billy was stricken with pneumonia and taken to the hospital. His condition was complicated by heart trouble and, since Torchy, giving attention to Billy, could not care for the Great Dane, the dog was placed in the kennel of a local veterinarian.

Billy passed away the evening of February 12th, and almost simultaneous with his departure from this life, the Great Dane commenced to howl inconsolably, something, Torchy says, the dog had never done before.

With the death of Billy, Mrs. Connors was busy with the details of arranging to take her husband's body back to Indiana for burial. She phoned the veterinarian to see if he would continue to care for the dog until she returned. He said that he would and that the Great Dane was fine except that she had been howling a lot. Torchy left Pueblo, and the following Monday morning, less than a week after Billy's demise, she learned that the veterinarian had found the Great Dane dead in the kennel. He told her that he was completely at a loss to determine the cause of her death since she had been entirely healthy.

Torchy, in remarking upon this occurrence, said: "I had heard of such things but never gave them any serious thought before. However, from now on, I will always believe there is some connection with the canine world and ours, which we do not understand."

A woman, housewife and mother, wrote me from the West, requesting anonymity, but giving me several graphic accounts of what she termed "out-of-the-body" experiences.

"When this first happened to me, I was terrified. I had never heard of people going out of their bodies and I thought something had gone wrong with my nervous system. I would remember going differ-ent places—out of this world. Some places were so gorgeous of color that I thought I was in a fairy land and others were as of this world. I always seemed to know that the people I visited were dead. Many were friends and relatives that I knew. This is how I found out that I actually must be visiting another world . . .

"One night, I left my body and visited my grandmother, and a boy I had gone to school with was on the street with some other people. When I woke up, I exclaimed to myself: 'How could Jimmy be there? He isn't dead!'

"A few days later, I received a letter from my girl friend and she said that this boy had been killed in an accident at a logging camp. At the time of my dream, or whatever you would call this experience, I didn't know he was dead.

"One night, I was out of my body and I thought I would try to awaken my husband. I went directly to him. He couldn't see me and I kept trying to get his attention but it just wasn't any use so I went back into my bedroom. My body was in bed and I got in it, I don't know how, although I always feel a jerking sensation at the back of my neck. I can't understand why my husband didn't see me because I've heard that people are seen, sometimes, in this form. However, I know that he doesn't believe in these things, so perhaps that is why he can't see me.

"I also want to tell you that I have lots of dreams that come true. My grandmother was the same way. I feel her around me a lot. I hope you will keep this letter private as I don't want anyone to know these things. There was one time when I felt as though I wanted to tell friends that death was different from what they thought, and about the spirit world. They didn't believe me and thought I was crazy. I felt bad about it. Now, I never tell anyone, any more."

One Sunday, in the fall of 1936, while visiting a writer friend, Charlton Edholm, and his family, in Dobbs Ferry, New York, Mr. and Mrs. David Brooks, people I had never met, dropped in unexpectedly. Mr. Edholm commented that they shared my interest in the higher powers of mind and, during the conversation which developed on this subject, Mr. Brooks suddenly turned to me and requested that, since I knew nothing about them, he would like me to attempt an experiment to see if I received any "impressions" of what they were about to undertake.

I had never made a practice of telling people anything. What thoughts or impressions I had received on any occasion had been kept largely to myself, but Mr. Brooks was insistent. Wouldn't I, at least try to tell him something?

The Edholms were then residing in a fine old estate on top of a hill overlooking the Hudson River. It was growing dusk; there was a fire in the fireplace; the atmosphere of the old house and surroundings was unusually conducive to meditation. I suddenly felt like relaxing, making my mind receptive, and seeing what impressions, if any, might come to me. To my surprise, within a few moments, I had the strong feeling that a radical change was about to take place in the lives of this couple.

I turned to Mrs. Brooks and told her that it seemed to me she had just quit a job the night before which she had worked at for twelve and a half years, and that she was going west—to California. I said that her husband appeared to be going west, too, but that I had the strange impression they were not leaving together and each was going west for a different reason. Then, addressing Mr. Brooks, I told him that he intended to call upon an elderly man with the hope that he would finance some venture.

Confirming my statements as applied to them both, Mr. Brooks took a letter from his inside coat pocket, pressed it into my hands and requested me to tell him what impressions came to me from it. I protested that I had never had any experience trying to sense conditions or events from contact with any object associated with an individual, but my initial success in having given accurate information concerning their plans caused Mr. Brooks to urge my further experimentation.

In an exploratory spirit, I rubbed the envelope containing a letter between my palms. As I fixed my attention, with an inquiring attitude of mind as to the possible contents and any other facts that might pertain to the writer of this letter, definite feelings and reactions commenced to form in consciousness.

"This is a letter from the gentleman I said you were going to see out west," I stated. "But here is something peculiar—you've never met him. You are going to see him through a mutual friend who has told him about you and your project. It seems to me it has to do with excavations. And, if I am right, this gentleman tells you in this letter that his friend's endorsement of you is sufficient. He will gladly give you all his resources. He would give his life, if necessary, to help you accomplish your purpose."

As Mr. Brooks excitedly corroborated what I had just told him, I was seized with a sudden sharp pain in my right ear, which I associated with a condition in the body of the letter writer.

"Just a moment," I interrupted, "I'm getting a severe pain in my right ear. Is this man, at the present time, suffering from a mastoid?"

Mr. Brooks jumped to his feet. "Mr. Sherman," he said, "my friend has written me that this man he wants me to meet is now in the hospital . . . that he has a mastoid, as you say, but it's his *left* ear—not the right."

"Strange," I heard myself saying, "I still feel it's the *right* ear . . . but this man is seriously ill. You should get out to see him as soon as possible . . . I don't think he'll live long after you get there."

The Brooks made notations of my impressions, then took leave of the Edholms and myself, explaining that they had much to do in preparation for their departure. He was going west by car and she by train.

Some months later, a letter came to me from David Brooks, who said in part:

> "I thought you would be interested in knowing how correct your impressions were . . . you stated, as you remember, that my wife and I would go west but not together. This was true as I went

west on a mining proposition and Matilda went west, stopping off to visit her sister in Illinois before proceeding on to the coast . . .

"Then, the letter I asked you to hold in your hand was from Mr. E. R. Tufts of Phoenix. I was dumbfounded when you lifted your right hand to your right ear and tensed your face and said you felt considerable pain there. This information was not in the letter or in any letters from the old miner.

"What I held my tongue in my cheek over was that a Mr. H. Davis, who saw Tufts that summer in Phoenix, told me that Tufts had an abscess in his LEFT ear. I remember distinctly, at the time, wondering who was wrong and why you said RIGHT ear, as right ear was not in my mind.

"It is hardly likely that Mr. Davis would have told me left ear, and he made mention of it on several occasions, had he meant right ear. As you were perfectly honest in the way you recounted your impression, it is not probable that you were reading Davis' subconscious mind for you made no mention of Davis, nor had we.

"It seems apparent that you were securing impressions about a fact miles away, and while I do not wish to appear as offering explanations, it seems logical to me that your knowledge was being obtained from your contact with Tufts' letter. The vibrations it contained, though the letter did not refer to the writer's physical condition, gave you, in some way, the impression.

"Upon my arrival in Phoenix, Arizona, November 29th, 1936, I found Mr. Tufts lying on a bed, on his left side, with his RIGHT ear abscessed and nearly gone. You were right. He died the following Wednesday . . ."

While competing in the 100-mile motorcar race at Indianapolis on Labor Day, 1915, Eddie Rickenbacker had what is now known as a psychokinetic experience. He gives an account of it in the *American Magazine* for November, 1943. This is what he writes:

"My principal opponent, Johnny Aiken, had a faster car on the straightaway than I had, so I had to outdrive him on the curves. It was a dangerous track with concrete walls on each side. Hit one of those things and you're gone.

"At about the seventy-fifth mile, the wire spokes in my left rear wheel began to give. They cracked like rifle shots. I was grinding out about 125 miles an hour, and the crack of those spokes seemed, for a moment, like the sound of doom. The officials tried to flag me down; my own gang in the pit waved frantically for me to stop. But I wouldn't stop. I was giving Johnny a race; I wanted to win, and the race was almost over. If I stopped, I would be automatically disqualified. I wouldn't finish.

"Johnny whined past me on the straightaways; I snarled past him on the curves. It was neck-and-neck. Some of the other racers were dead or injured; I think one wreck was burning at the edge of the track. The crowd was yelling for me to stop. Then I felt the wheel begin to wobble.

"On the next to the last lap, the wheel was wobbling so dangerously that Johnny gallantly came up alongside as he passed me on the back stretch and signaled a warning. But still I did not stop.

"When the wheel collapsed, the tire blew and spun me toward the lower concrete wall. Then another tire blew and spun me back to the other wall. I had lost control completely, but the car did not hit either wall.

"When I finally stopped, after spreading rubber and wheels all over the track, I was standing on my four brake drums, still upright and grinning. The boys in the pit had the fright of their lives. I had lost the race. But I had discovered something which I still believe: As I roared down the last stretch, it came to me that I could control that machine with my mind, that I could hold it together with my mind, and that if it finally collapsed, I could run it with my mind It was a feeling of mastery, of supreme confidence. But it was real.

"If I had said such a thing then, the boys would have called me crazy. Even now I can't explain it. But I have been told that scientists now are investigating a phenomenon called psychokinetics, the control of mind over matter. It isn't new to me. I believe that if you think disaster, you will get it. Brood about death, and you will hasten your demise. Think positively and masterfully, with confidence and faith, and life will be more secure, more fraught with action, richer in achievement and experience.

"There are a lot of things about the human mind and soul that we don't know much about. We get glimpses of them in times of danger or suffering when we cross over the line of ordinary thought a little way."

Thousands of men and women, like Eddie Rickenbacker, at one time or another, have crossed over the line of ordinary thought a little way, and have discovered new mental powers awaiting them, ready to be exercised. Just as Science has revealed that another world exists beyond the supersonic barriers in the stratosphere, Man is now becoming increasingly aware that there is a vast new world of consciousness beyond the barrier which has been imposed by his five physical senses.

You have had a glimpse into the genuine extra sensory experiences of a few men and women, representative of the many, covering almost every variety of super normal phenomena pertaining to the past, present and future. No attempt has been made to evaluate or explain them in this chapter. The purpose herein has been to give you a panoramic knowledge of their nature and scope, and perhaps to enable you to identify and classify similar experiences you have had in your own life or that have occurred to those near and dear to you.

In succeeding chapters, you will be told, insofar as is possible, how to develop your own powers of extra sensory perception, and how to utilize them in a way that can have a practical, beneficial and protective influence in your everyday life.

THREE

The Power of
Meditation and Prayer

Y OU SHOULD now be fairly well impressed with the fact, if
you have not considered such evidence before, that you possess in your individual consciousness, undeveloped powers of unimagined scope. A mere review of the case histories just recounted should
be sufficient to suggest to any thinking person that our knowledge of
the human mind and its potentialities is still in infancy. But, like elec-
tricity, the fundamental nature of which is yet beyond comprehension,
we are beginning to discover that, if we can develop and assume certain attitudes and states of mind, definite results can be attained.

Today there is increasing recognition of the fact that Man creates in mind the world in which he lives. You are basically what you
think you are. You are, in any present moment, the result of all your
past thinking. The ancients said it all in one sentence when they declared, "As a man thinketh in his mind and in his heart, so is he." Every experience you have had is recorded in your mind and continues
to exist in consciousness, whether you can recall it at will or not—
the good thoughts and happenings with the bad. And, since there
is a universal mental law that "like always attracts like," your good

thoughts have attracted good things to you and your bad thoughts, bad things.

When an idea takes form in consciousness and goes out from mind, it seeks to externalize itself and become manifest in the world without. This is the way in which your dreams of today become the realities of tomorrow. But what you visualize in mind through meditation must be vitalized by faith and crystallized by prayer so that your Creative Power within will be activated to the point of magnetizing conditions around you and attracting, in due course of time, the circumstances and resources necessary to the realization of your desires. You must believe wholeheartedly in whatever attainment you picture for yourself and put forth every earnest effort toward its achievement, if you expect or hope for an answer to prayer.

There is profound truth in the old adage, "God helps those who help themselves." The laws of God will not work for you unless you work for them.

There is the story of an old mountaineer who was stretched out on the ground in front of his run-down shack. A passing motorist suddenly stopped and cried out: "Hey, Mister! Your house is on fire! Hadn't you better be doing something about it?"

"I am doing somethin' about it!" replied the mountaineer, without moving a muscle. "Ever since the fire started, I've been prayin' for rain!"

The God of this universe does not change the laws of Nature to suit your specific needs and purposes. Nevertheless, millions of humans are unthinkingly calling upon God to serve them in this manner. They have been taught that faith alone should be sufficient to produce results. But blind faith is never answered. It is mere mechanical lip-service which has no effect whatsoever upon the God-given Creative Power in consciousness. This must be reached and activated by right visualization, supported by an exercise of knowing faith that what you desire will come to pass, in time, if you put forth every physical and mental effort toward its attainment.

Your physical body is the instrument through which what you picture in mind becomes manifest in your outer life. Your contact with your body is established and maintained through *feeling*. Every thought you have experienced from your first moment of conscious awareness in this body has had feeling behind it but, since consciousness, itself, is *feeling*, you have actually had a sensory awareness from the moment of conception and the taking on of form. Much that you have felt or sensed in your present organism has never reached the threshold of consciousness. It, nevertheless, is playing its influential part in your emotionalized reactions to everything that happens to you. There is a deeper side of you that is always aware of what is going on, in and about you.

Like the old analogy of the iceberg, there is only one-eighth of you above the surface of consciousness and seven-eighths remains submerged in the Great Subconscious. What seems to be buried there, contains your emotional reaction to every experience you have ever had, good or bad, constructive or destructive, from the moment of your existence here. What shows above the surface of your life is what you have made of yourself, or failed to make, as a result of your past thoughts and acts. Since each act has been the outgrowth of thought, it is actually the externalization of that thought. But all thinking, every movement of consciousness, is dictated by *feeling*.

How you feel about any person or thing or condition or event or idea, determines what your reaction to that person or thing or condition or event or idea will be. For this reason, you can readily realize how easily the mind of man can be played upon by an emotional appeal to his racial or established hates and prejudices, and a feeling reaction aroused, often of sufficient intensity to blot out man's reason and influence him against the exercise of fair and unbiased judgment.

As a creature of Free Will, you are charged by the cosmos, which gave you *being*, with the responsibility for bringing these all-powerful feelings under conscious control and direction. Unbridled feelings of hate, resentment, lust, greed, fear, worry, jealousy, prejudice and the like can destroy any man and all men. But feeling, in itself, is neutral, capable of being changed at the will of any sentient being, and serving either constructive or destructive ends.

When the feeling of hate is changed to the feeling of love, the law of repulsion has then been replaced by the law of attraction. Harmony never invites discord but out of discord, harmony often evolves. This is because the basic principles of the universe are founded upon law and order, and where discord is found, it is with things and beings temporarily out of harmony with the laws of their nature.

You may be certain, therefore, that wherever and whenever you find discord in your life, it has either been attracted to you or created, directly or indirectly, by some wrong emotional or mental reaction to the life happening. Nothing can take place in your outer world that is not a reflection in whole or in part of a thought and feeling that has come from the Great Within.

When you say, or everyone has said, "I was afraid that was going to happen," you are confessing that, through feelings of fear, worry and apprehension, you have pictured yourself having an unhappy experience and, by such emotionalized picturing, have set up the cause in consciousness which has produced this exact effect in your outer world.

This being true, it becomes unmistakably clear that the fearless, positive picturing of some worthwhile achievement can and will activate the Creative Power in your subconscious in such a manner as to materialize, in time, whatever has been visualized. Spasmodically, you have been doing this all your life, your mental pictures with strong, confident feelings behind them, have produced good results, while your wrong mental pictures, with disturbed, uncertain feelings behind them, have brought to pass wrong results.

You are not, as many might like to believe, a creature of circumstance. You create your own circumstances. Luck, in the usual sense of this word, does not exist in a universe which is ruled inexorably by the laws of cause and effect. Every particle in the cosmos is in motion at all times and is influenced or changed by, and in turn influences and changes every other particle with which it comes in contact. The degree of this influence or change at any given moment is determined by the length of duration and the intensity of the association. What is true of particles is also true of individual intelligences, mind repercussing upon mind as humans make contact with one another.

Whether you realize it or not, you have an affinity in consciousness with every human who has ever lived, who now lives, or who will live on this earth. In your own subconscious, you partake of the race consciousness which has contributed the backdrop for your arrival on the stage of life. From the moment of your own self-conscious existence, you have added and are adding your individualized thought impressions to the race consciousness. In time to come, long after you have departed this plane of being, the thoughts you have left behind will be having their proportionate subconscious effect upon the thought patterns of entities now unborn. There is no end and beginning in the Great Subconscious. It extends in both directions, past and future, from this present moment.

You have your awareness in what you have conceived to be different segments of time, represented by seconds, minutes, hours, days, weeks, months and years. This concept of time suits the convenience of your five physical senses and your ordinary external activities on this planet. It is quite obviously not universe time. It is time in its most limited sense because the Subconscious part of you, when freed of the influence of your conscious mind, knows no limitation either as to time or space.

During my experiments in telepathy with Sir Hubert Wilkins, when he was in the north polar regions searching for the lost Russian fliers, and I was in my study in New York City, separated by over three thousand miles, time and space were eliminated in consciousness. Since telepathy is the transmission of a thought from the subconscious mind of a sender to the subconscious mind of a receiver, such communication is not inhibited by the usual, limited conscious concept of time and space.

Once I had completely relaxed my physical body and made myself temporarily unaware of it, I could, by turning the attention of my conscious mind inward, quietly and expectantly await the reception in mental picture or strong feeling form of impressions from the mind of Wilkins who would usually be concentrating upon me at the appointed times. I found, significantly, that it was helpful for me to suggest to my inner mind, "Determine for me what has happened to Wilkins this day or is happening to him now," as a means of directing these extra sensory faculties to confine their operations within this span of time. Otherwise, I would be apt to tune in, having contacted Wilkins' subconscious, on events which had occurred to him some days, months or even years before, since a record of all these happenings continues to exist in consciousness.

Try to conceive of the millions upon millions upon millions of thought impressions, covering all past experiences which you and every human are carrying in consciousness! This will help you to understand the difficulties to be encountered by any sensitized receiver in trying to segregate or pick out any specific thought forms from this great reservoir. But when you direct your mind's attention to a certain point, it seeks identification with that point and, once identification is established, you are made aware of what exists at that point. This can be likened to radar which can now get a "fix" on an object in space and direct a plane or a guided missile unerringly to it.

And yet, beyond the remarkable workings of your own thought processes, and residing in some incomprehensible manner as a part of your own subconscious, is the God Consciousness. It speaks to you, at times, and you have been fleetingly conscious of it through what you call your *intuition*. It never obtrudes; it never compels, it only presents, usually in critical moments, flashing but definite *feelings* of what you should or should not do, which you may or may not have developed the ability to recognize and to act upon for your own good.

God, the Great Intelligence, is co-existent with everything that is, through His eternal, infallible laws on every level of *being*. And you can develop, if you desire, through meditation, a form of *spiritualized telepathy* by which your mind is brought in attunement, for want of any better way to describe it, with the Mind, the Consciousness, the Intelligence that is God.

This does not mean that you contact God or His Principles on the highest level of His Being, but on the level of your own attainment. And God, because of His Eternal Attributes, must always remain the Eternal Magnet, drawing each evolving, individualized consciousness toward Him, revealing more and more of His Higher Nature to man as man consciously develops an awareness of that Higher Nature within him.

It can thus be seen that God, the Great Intelligence, cannot be a personal God, as man has conceived Him, in man's image, a glorified Being seated upon a throne in some imagined heavenly place in the sky. Through the centuries, the spiritual leaders who declared that,

"The Kingdom of God is within" are now known to have had the true concept of this universe of *Being*. The Kingdom consists of the immutable laws of God which extend, to all who obey them, Infinite compassion and bounteous rewards. God is not sitting in judgment upon you; you are sitting in judgment upon yourself. God's Laws are so designed, with a wisdom forever beyond understanding, that they automatically punish every thing and every intelligence in the universe that disobeys them, however seemingly insignificant the offense, in whatever form of life, high or low, that offense may be committed.

The God Presence within is the guarantee of eternal sustenance to all life, although the forms of life, in infinite planes of being, may be subject to eternal change as they evolve ever upward, ever seeking a closer affinity with the Father-Mother of all creation.

By accepting this profoundly enlarged concept of God, you do not lose any sense of personal relationship to Him. Instead, you come into a feeling of intimacy and closeness utterly impossible of attainment on the basis of any other concept.

Your reason should tell you that you and millions of other surviving human souls cannot dwell in the physical presence of a God in a heavenly state and spend an eternity singing praises to Him. There could be nothing intimate and personal in such an association and no God, worthy of the Name, would wish His creatures to devote an eternity dedicated to nothing but worshipful adoration of Him.

The concept of hosts of souls assembled before the throne of God may make a sublime picture for the unthinking mind, but few could ever get close enough to such a God to gain any individual, loving recognition or personal attention. Particularly would this be true if one would take into consideration the inconceivable multitude of surviving creatures from other planets, no less the children of God and no less entitled to claim a place by His side. You cannot deny to other deserving creatures what you would rightfully expect for yourself, and you can readily see that a God of such limited concept could not make Himself personally available to His myriads of surviving creatures at any time or in any place.

The day must come when religion, in the light of man's expanding consciousness and increasing awareness of the God Presence within, will put aside its well-intentioned but outmoded creeds and dogmas and permit Man to find God for himself in the kingdom of his own mind and heart.

You can begin to experience, through medium of a technique of meditation, to be set forth herein, a knowing attunement with the God Consciousness. You can, through intelligently directed prayers, awaken higher sensory powers within you which will make it increasingly possible for the God Power within to offer guidance and protection to you through the faculty of your intuition.

God can become a Personal Being in your life and you can commune with Him in consciousness. When you pray, you will be praying to a God Presence within you— not without. There will no longer be a feeling of aloneness, a feeling that you may be appealing to a God in some glorified form, in a place remote from you, Who may or may not be listening to your prayer.

When the realization comes to you that a part of God, the Great Intelligence, actually indwells you, in that moment will be born a deep and abiding assurance of basic peace and security. Then will sweep over you a new sense of inner strength which you can put to work in your life in direct accordance with the degree of faith you develop in this God Power and in yourself. Nothing is ever accomplished by faith alone. It must be accompanied by works. The statement is universally true that "Faith without works is dead." You cannot impress this God Consciousness with words. They must be supported by an earnest, even burning desire to be worthy of that for which you are praying and a sincere willingness to put forth every effort in thankful appreciation for the functioning of the God Power in your behalf.

God, the Great Intelligence, can never be kidded. You cannot get something for nothing on a spiritual level any more than you can get it on a physical or mental plane. It will require devotion of time each day, preferably night and morning, to develop the power of meditation and to attune yourself to the God Consciousness, through prayer. At the start, unless you have had previous experience in this way of thinking, you can expect to encounter some difficulties in relaxing your physical body, in gaining emotional control, in making your conscious mind passive, and in fixing your attention, to the exclusion of everything else, upon the thought content and meaning and purpose of the prayers you may wish to express.

The end of each day, just before retiring, is usually the best time to prepare your body and your mind for attunement with the God Consciousness. You must be emotionally and mentally free from anything that might make a demand upon you. This kind of freedom is seldom possible during the day's activities when your mind is filled with duties and responsibilities, and your emotions are reacting to the stresses and strains of average human life.

In time to come, when you have developed emotional and mental control, you will be able to release your nerve tensions, quiet any disturbed feelings in consciousness and draw upon the God Power within to serve you in moments of great need. This may not now be possible to you because of the existence of certain strong fears and worries which so take possession of your conscious mind, as you face different situations and problems, that you lack the strength of will and concentration to take your attention from the outer world and to fix it upon the world within. Could you do this, you would receive through your intuition, an almost immediate answer to many difficulties.

It is important for you to realize that your Conscious mind functions as your reasoning, guessing, wondering, calculating, assimilating mind which contacts your outer world through medium of your five physical senses. It reports, in mental picture and feeling form, whatever happens in this outer world, and your reaction to these happenings in consciousness determines your state of body and mind at any given moment.

The conclusions you arrive at through reason are based upon its evaluation of your past experience and acquired knowledge as applied to the situation at hand.

When a new decision is reached, reason has extracted the wisdom from past successes and failures and activated the Creative Power within to produce a logical answer in the form of a definite feeling and conviction of what should be done.

The more abstract the reasoning, the more necessary it is for the reasoning faculty to call upon the Creative Power with its amazing ability to correlate all past accumulated mental and emotional impressions on all allied phases of the problem under consideration. Once this is done, the Creative Power sorts out just the factors needed, like a calculating machine, bringing them forth in a new arrangement which takes the form of a new idea or theory when it reaches outer consciousness.

When reason is not applied to your decisions and actions in life and when you permit yourself to be ruled by feeling alone, the Creative Power within responds *impersonally* to the dictates of your feelings, good or bad, and starts materializing for you in your outer life whatever you have pictured through your desires or fears.

Remember, the nature of events always changes as the nature of thought is altered. This Creative Power in your mind constantly responds to whatever mental pictures you give it and magnetizes or demagnetizes conditions around you in accordance with the intensity of the desires and fears associated with whatever you visualize. It does not discriminate between your good and your bad thoughts. It will materialize the one as quickly as the other if there is the same emotional drive behind it. Consciousness is feeling and feeling is power—tremendous power—which can be used at any time, constructively or destructively, dependent upon the free will choice of the entity.

It is therefore imperative that you give conscious attention to the development, control and direction of this power in your everyday life. This can only be done in periods of meditation wherein you reflect upon your past acts and thoughts and evaluate them impersonally as a means of determining your strengths and weaknesses and deciding what you can and must do to improve your ways of thinking and living. Untold numbers of men and women awaken, after many wasted years, to the realization of what they might have thought and done, long ago, and how vastly, for the better, this would have altered their lives.

No mind can conceive the stupendous loss to humanity in "what might have been." Could every human have gained sufficient understanding of himself and his true relationship to the God Power within, and could each human have made full and intelligent use of this Power in his life, the world would long since have been transformed into a heaven on earth and all human creatures would now be in constant conscious attunement with the God Power within. Unhappily, as yet, only one in thousands has raised his thinking to this level of awareness.

But you, if you are willing to put forth the meditative, prayerful effort, will be able to experience the existence of this God Consciousness in your own mind.

To still the voice of emotion and to listen to the voice of the higher self within requires complete physical relaxation of your body and the passivity of your conscious mind. If it has not been your habit to practice meditation for a few minutes each day, you will need to set aside the most convenient time and the most secluded place for such exercise. Life is ordinarily so ordered that few humans regularly have the opportunity to get off by themselves.

In fact, many humans are actually afraid to face themselves, and fill every waking moment in association with others, often resorting to extreme measures to avoid being alone. These individuals have become so emotionally disturbed that they have severed all awareness of the God Presence within and fear the barrenness of their own inner selves. As they contemplate themselves apart from the life about them, upon which they have fixed their attention, they experience such a frightening feeling of nothingness that they constantly, almost frantically, strive to escape from themselves. These efforts to escape often take the form of narcotics, or alcoholism or a series of unsatisfying sex adventures, or any and all types of experiences which may serve to drug the senses and keep such a person from any personal reflection.

But there is only one road that can lead these distraught people, or any humans out of the wilderness of muddled feelings and thoughts, and this is the road that leads to the intersection of Man's consciousness with the God Consciousness within. At this point, Man's will becomes God's Will, and the two wills interjoin so that the Power of God becomes manifest through Man.

Man, by himself, is truly nothing, and he senses this fact when he is functioning through his lower nature, so that he derives no lasting pleasure from his thoughts and acts on this level. He knows, instinctively, that he is cut off from a higher self within which does not approve of his uncontrolled expression of mind and feelings.

How to get back or to make contact, perhaps for the first time, with this higher self and the God Consciousness, is Man's greatest problem. It has been Man's Number One problem throughout the ages. God, the Great Intelligence, has never compelled this union. It has been left, and always will be left, to Man's free will choice. Each human must find God in his own way but, once found, this God Power serves all humans, so attuned, in equal measure, in direct accordance with the degree of their attunement.

Should members of your family, or those with whom you reside, not be in sympathy with your desire for privacy at certain times, you must either request that they respect this desire, or seek some place where you can be reasonably certain that you will not be intruded upon. You must be free of any apprehension of interference during the time you intend to devote to meditation. Without this assurance, it will be impossible to completely relax body and mind.

If your interest in meditation is shared by husband or wife or friend in whom you confide, you must still retain absolute privacy in your own meditation since this function of consciousness is strictly between the real you and the God Power within. At the very same time, your wife or husband or friend may be attuning their minds to the identical God Consciousness which indwells them, and deriving their specific benefits therefrom. It is always stimulating and helpful to know that friends or loved ones are sincerely interested in developing themselves along with you. The more you associate with those who are endeavoring to raise the quality of their own thinking, the more will you be inspired to persist in extending your own awareness.

Should you select an evening time for meditation after the day's work is done, and you have nothing else in mind but the thought of retirement, such conditions should be conducive to results. The time you set for meditation may be earlier or later on different nights, just so your mind is entirely free when you arrive at this moment.

Seat yourself in a restful chair or recline upon a sofa or bed in whatever position is most natural and comfortable for you to relax. Direct your conscious mind's attention to your body and you will be made aware of the nerve tensions which have built up throughout the day and which now need to be released by an act of mind. See a mental picture of yourself letting go of the feelings which have been reflected in these nerve tensions. Visualize the chair or sofa or bed, whatever is supporting your body, assuming the complete weight of it. You will sense, almost instantly, a feeling of buoyancy and lightness, and, as you do so, dismiss all feelings of worry and fear and apprehension by an act of will. Say to yourself, "I now let go of everything in body and in mind that has been disturbing me in consciousness."

Without straining, without forcing, as you let the physical and mental tensions drop from you, turn the attention of your now passive conscious mind inward and let it rest upon the visualized focal point of a blank, white screen or a soothing area of darkness, whichever is easier for you to create. This exercise, often enough repeated, simple as it is, will enable you to withdraw your conscious mind's attention from the world without and fix it upon the world within. When you have accomplished this and have discovered that you can hold such a mental attitude for appreciable moments, you will then be ready to crystallize your thoughts through prayer which, in turn, with the impact of deep feeling behind them, supported by the vital energy of faith, will carry you to the threshold of God Consciousness.

Prayer, to be effective, must be meaningful. It must be so designed that your inner mind grasps the full intent and purpose of the prayer and is so moved by your deeply expressed thought and feeling that the highest centers of your being are touched and the Creative Power within is impulsed to act in your behalf.

Your higher sensory faculties are the channels through which the God Consciousness is reached. They exist ready to function, just beyond the outermost limits of the five physical senses, and the key that unlocks the invisible door to these powers is your *faith*.

This faith, as the Bible has stated, is truly "the substance of things hoped for, the evidence of things not seen." You must believe that what you desire, as expressed in prayer, you not only deserve but have the power to receive. This faith must be positive, expectant, unwavering, or it will not energize your God-given Creative Power which must be activated before the prayer, itself, can be answered. Utter sincerity, unselfishness, simplicity and directness should be the attitude in which you approach prayer. You should carry into each meditation the conviction that what you are about to pray for has already been realized by you in mind and requires only to be vitalized by attunement with the God Power within to become, eventually, a reality in your outer life.

Often, when you have no specific desire for which to pray, it will prove a physical, mental and spiritual tonic to you just to relax body and mind and to devote a few moments dwelling knowingly in the presence of the God Consciousness. But, at present, you probably are in need of the approach in prayer which can enable you to make conscious contact with this God Power within.

Once this contact is established, God, the Great Intelligence, becomes *personal* to you. Your act of attunement has personalized God in your consciousness and your life, and, ever more, as you maintain your awareness of the God Power within, this increasingly comforting and inspiring feeling of personal kinship with God will grow. Thus, while God's Eternal Laws and Principles are impersonal as they apply to all forms of life everywhere, as they operate in and through you, they become intimate and personal and soul-satisfying.

Aside from such specific prayers as you will wish to offer up according to your needs, there are five basic prayers which, if earnestly and meaningfully expressed, can be depended upon to put you in touch with the God Consciousness, and to bring you the answers that you seek. Each prayer is designed to accomplish a great fundamental purpose in your life.

The five prayers might be described as:

1. Prayer of Inspiration
2. Prayer of Adjustment
3. Prayer of Re-Creation
4. Prayer of Abundance
5. Prayer of Attunement

Each prayer should be studied so that you have a full comprehension of its import before giving expression to it in a period of meditation. Each prayer, you will find, first prepares the consciousness for reception of the prayerfully expressed desire through a stated recognition of your need to put forth every physical and mental effort in support of the request you are presenting to the God Power within. In this manner, your co-partnership with God is established through your willingness to support your faith in Him by your works.

Observe now, this approach to God in the "Prayer of Inspiration":

Our Father—
Eternal Source of All Power and Wisdom and Intelligence—
Cause me to realize that I must prepare my mind
If I would consciously receive and apply to my life
The knowledge and guidance you are always ready
To impart from your Indwelling Presence.

As you give expression to the preceding lines, focus your complete attention upon them and let yourself feel the full impact of their thought and meaning in your consciousness. Let there exist a great yearning in you, as you say, "Cause me to realize that I must prepare my mind . . ." because you reach God-ward only through such feelings, intelligently expressed. You are actually creating that for which you are praying in consciousness and planting the seeds for progressive development and unfoldment as you give utterance to each line in this prayer:

Cause me to understand that, as a creature of free will and free choice,
I am never compelled but am always offered
The opportunity to follow Your instructions
Which may come to me in the form of inner urges, impulses, impressions, feelings and ideas.
Cause me to know that, through what I call Intuition,
You answer prayer,
Speaking to me through the Voice of Conscience
Which always discriminates between wrong and right thinking, feeling and action.

Herein is contained a stated awareness of the action and interaction between your consciousness and the God Consciousness. By putting this process into words and giving conscious recognition to it, in prayer, you help bring this desired condition to pass. What you have felt, instinctively, to be true cannot become actively true until you give conscious recognition to it. Because your inner mind responds to the suggestion of your conscious mind, once you have feelingly declared: "Cause me to know that, through what I call 'Intuition,' You answer prayer . . ." you have thereafter developed an expectancy in consciousness for you to be served increasingly by intuition.

And now, as you proceed further, you set up new concepts which will open up vital avenues of mind and activate, even more, your higher sensory powers to the end that a knowing relationship can be established between yourself and the God Power within.

> As I pray, with Faith,
> In full willingness to put forth every effort toward attainment on my part,
> I know that this mental attitude activates the Creative Power within,
> And that this Power magnetizes conditions around me
> And begins to attract to me the resources and circumstances and even the people I need,
> To enable this prayed-for-desire to materialize in my outer life,
> In this full realization,
> I now pray that the channels of my mind will always be open
> To receive Inspiration and Guidance and Protection From Your Indwelling Presence.
> Amen

This last statement and petition concludes the "Prayer of Inspiration" and condenses, as you now realize, the entire machinery of mind which must be put into operation to enable God, the Great Intelligence, to work creatively through you to help you secure a definite, satisfying, deserved answer to genuine prayer.

The "Prayer of Inspiration," in its entirety, is as follows:

> Our Father—
> Eternal Source of All Power and Wisdom and Intelligence—
> Cause me to realize that I must prepare my mind
> If I would consciously receive and apply to my life
> The knowledge and guidance You are always ready to impart from Your Indwelling Presence.

Cause me to understand that, as a creature of free will and free choice,

I am never compelled but am always offered

The opportunity to follow Your Instructions

Which may come to me in the form of inner urges, impulses, impressions, feelings and ideas.

Cause me to know that, through what I call Intuition,

You answer prayer,

Speaking to me through the Voice- of Conscience

Which always discriminates between wrong and right thinking, feeling and action.

As I pray, with Faith,

In full willingness to put forth every effort toward attainment on my part,

I know that this mental attitude activates the Creative Power within,

And that this Power magnetizes conditions around me

And begins to attract to me the resources and circumstances and even the people I need,

To enable this prayed-for-desire to materialize in my outer life,

In this full realization,

I now pray that the channels of my mind will always be open

To receive Inspiration and Guidance and Protection

From Your Indwelling Presence.

You can see now that true prayer is far more than a petition to the God Power within to do everything for you with no effort or responsibility on your part. It is a dedication of your entire being expressed through faith in yourself as well as in God. This faith, properly exercised, enables you to rise above all conflicts in consciousness which might otherwise obstruct an answer to prayer such as your fears, worries, doubts, inferiorities, resentments, prejudices and other emotional disturbances.

But the most effective prayer is one in which you pledge yourself, before God, to eliminate from your consciousness and your life, insofar as is possible, all that you recognize should not exist there. Such an attitude makes it easier and easier for the God Power to work in and through you since it will encounter less and less resistance from wrong thoughts and feelings.

The "Prayer of Adjustment" is designed for the purpose of aiding you in overcoming any prejudices and antagonisms you may have toward others. You will have taken a great step forward in your own evolution of mind and soul when you have accomplished this. Concentrate upon each line until you have extracted the full meaning from it as applied to yourself.

When using this prayer in your periods of meditation, resolve that this new tolerance and understanding of your fellow humans will so permeate your consciousness that it will contribute toward a more friendly, understanding association with all others under any and all circumstances. This may be the most difficult of all prayers for you to enter into, conscientiously, since it involves necessary basic changes in your own mind and heart.

But, if you really desire to improve conditions in the world about you, this improvement must first begin within yourself.

This is the "Prayer of Adjustment":

Our Father—
Creator of all races and colors of men—Cause me to see
In them, aside from all seeming differences,
What I see in myself:
The same basic feelings and desires,
The same dreams and ambitions,
The same love of home and family,
The same inexpressible urge for a deeper understanding of self,
And a knowledge of God and the Universe.
Cause me to realize
That, however high or low in the scale of development my fellow
    humans may be,
I bear a kinship to them of whatever race and color,
As children of the same Creator.
Cause me to understand
That, since a part of God, the Great Intelligence, indwells each
    human soul,

We are each partakers of Your "I AM" Consciousness,

In the process of evolving our Souls by the manner in which we
react to the associative experiences, We are having on this
earth.

Cause me to sense

The harm I am doing to myself by permitting age-old prejudices
against any race or color or individual

To continue to exist in consciousness,

Thus keeping me from acceptance of the true brotherhood of
Man under the Fathership of God.

Cause me to be tolerant

Of the imperfections of my human brothers,

As I would wish them to be tolerant of me and my shortcomings,

Let me resolve

To apply this tolerance in relation to loved ones and friends in
particular,

With the determination to change those unhappy qualities in myself which need changing,

As a first step toward inviting a similar change in others.

To this end,

I pray for the strength, the patience, the spirit and the will,

To carry me forward, each day, in the service of my fellow humans,

As my contribution toward a happier life and a better world tomorrow.

Amen

Health of body as well as mind is essential to happy, successful
living. At any given moment of any day or night, more humans are
probably praying to God to heal them of various illnesses and injuries
than all other manner of petitions. It is characteristic of many humans
to turn to God only when faced with some dire emergency or bodily
affliction. They give little or no consideration to the fact that they have
brought most of these illnesses and injuries upon themselves through
wrong thinking and conduct. Despite this, without any expressed desire to change their thoughts and actions which have caused God's
Laws to act against them, they appeal to God, the Great Intelligence,

to restore their health and to liberate them from their physical and mental difficulties. Few, under these circumstances, receive a satisfying answer to prayer. Those, however, who recognize that the cause of their troubles exists largely within themselves and who promise God, through prayer, that they will strive to correct these causes, bring about such a change in consciousness that it is reflected, often at once, in a greatly improved physical condition. Countless instantaneous healings and remarkable recuperations have occurred as a result of prayer.

This "Prayer of Re-Creation" is designed to give you a conscious awareness of the functioning of the Creative Power within as it applies to the re-creation of any and all body imperfections which have developed through wrong emotional and mental reactions to life experiences.

Give the contents of this prayer profound study until its concepts have become a conviction within you. This conviction, carried over into your meditation period, will so strengthen your faith that the Creative Power will be activated and set to work at that point or points in your body or mind which require re-creation. Live in the expectancy of better health, in the confidence that the clearing of wrong thoughts and emotions from mind and heart has provided the foundation for your recovery. Close out all doubts and apprehensions so that the creative process, once started, will not be impeded.

This is your "Prayer of Re-Creation":

Our Father—
Designer and Creator of the body in which I dwell— In and
    through which I live and move and have my being,
Cause me to realize
That the perfect pattern of my body is contained in my conscious-
    ness—
That anything less than perfect which has manifested or does
    manifest in this body,
Has been the result of my wrong thinking and wrong operation of
    Your Universal Laws.
Should my body have been imperfect at birth,
It has still been the result of human causations and not by any
    Divine decree.

Cause me to realize

That Your Creative Power which fashioned this body,

Is still resident in my consciousness, ready to serve me at any time
of need;

That I, as a creature of Free Will, now have control of this Creative
Power,

And may direct it for my own good or ill, dependent upon the
nature and character of my thoughts and feelings.

In full realization of this,

I now call upon Your Creative Power within me,

To correct and eliminate any and all body imperfections.

As I do so,

I know that Re-Creation is taking place,

In every cell and nerve and gland and tissue and organ,

In direct accordance with the degree of my vision and my faith.

Amen

Residing, as you do, in a world which makes constant economic demands upon you, one of your recurring problems may have to do
with lack of resources to meet your needs. In times of adversity and
scarcity it often seems that there is no escape from this condition. It
is emotionally easier for the mind to picture less rather than more.
Fear of lack is one of our deepest fears. Could we overcome this
and bring ourselves in attunement with God's Law of Abundance,
it would banish lack from our lives. But, unfortunately, lack is created by fears, worries, doubts and other destructive emotions which
cause us to picture the possibility of failure more strongly than success, and to lose sight of activities, associations and goals which could
lead us to the opportunities and resources we need. The world is out
of balance because humans are out of balance in their thoughts and
feelings.

You can restore your own balance in your attitude toward the
problem of lack, through this "Prayer of Abundance":

Our Father—

Creator of the Universe and the Boundless Substances—

From which all things and all life are made. Cause me to realize

That there is no lack in any needed resource, At any time or in
any place,

Except as I create that lack through my own wrong or limited
thinking.

Help me to fix in my mind

The assurance that there is an answer to my every need

Through Your Creative Power which resides in my consciousness,

And which responds to the nature of my fears or desires,

Let me be constantly aware

That my possession of little or much will be in proportion to my
over-all concept of scarcity and plenty.

I thank you, Dear Father, for the Law of Abundance,

Which I am free to operate

At any time, by development within me, of the "consciousness of
Abundance,"

A consciousness which pictures gain instead of loss,

Success instead of failure,

And which profits from every experience, good or bad,

Converting all into a means of attracting

What is best for me and my dear ones.

This is the attitude, Dear Father,

Which I now assume and maintain

To the end that my material needs will be amply cared for,

From this moment on.

Amen

Knowing attunement with the God Consciousness comes to you
as you develop control of your Conscious mind and emotions, and attain a state of receptivity capable of receiving and interpreting the testimony of your extra sensory faculties. It is through these faculties that
you sense the existence of the God Consciousness within. Therefore,
more than any other prayer, the "Prayer of Attunement" is designed to
help you come into a full conscious awareness of your personal relationship to God, the Father, in consciousness.

The feeling is unmistakable and indescribable when it comes. It is
an all-possessing quieting, calming, profoundly assuring, comforting,
unquestioning, inspiring sensation, impossible to put into words. It is a

feeling you cannot hold long at a time in your conscious mind but one to which you can return, time and again, for sustenance and guidance.

Do not expect bells to ring and guns to boom when contact is made with the God Consciousness. This is an inner experience, not an outer. But no experience you can have on this earth can mean more to you, because you will know, as you say in your "Prayer of Attunement":

Our Father—
Whose power resides within me,
Of whose consciousness I am a part,
In Whom I move and have my being—
Cause me to know that
You, my Creator,
Have instilled in me the power and the wisdom
To create for myself the world in which I live;
To deliver myself from the evil of my own wrong thinking;
To lift myself from where I am to where I wish to be
By releasing all feelings of fear and resentment and hate,
By forgiving others as I would be forgiven,
And by keeping myself in attunement with Your Indwelling Presence.
I thank You, Dear Father,
For the Inner assurance that I am never alone,
That You are always with me,
And that I may turn to You for guidance and protection whenever
    I feel the need—
For You are the Power and the Wisdom and the Love
That will abide with me Forever.
Amen

These five prayers, repeated thoughtfully and with great sincerity of purpose and feeling, as often as needed, will bring about, eventually, such a change in your own consciousness as to change for the better every phase of your life.

There is tremendous power in meditation and in prayer. Are you willing to devote the time and the effort to develop it? If you are, an unlimited horizon of enfoldment and achievement lies before you.

FOUR

The Power of Intuition

MANY MEN AND WOMEN have written me saying, "I never believed in telepathy or precognition before—but now that it has happened to me, I *know* there's something to it!"

Experience will always be the best "convincer." This also applies to your contacting the God Consciousness. You will know, when this happens, and all the scoffing and skepticism of others who have not yet had this great inner experience will leave you unmoved.

It is highly important that you maintain an open-minded attitude, ready to accept what reason and intuition tell you is the truth, regardless of the opinions of others. Test out in your own life, whenever possible, what appeals to you as truth but which you feel requires a little more proving.

My experiments in extra sensory perception with Sir Hubert Wilkins taught me much about the operation of mind. These experiments revealed many significant facts with respect to thought, feeling and consciousness, and I am still studying and evaluating the results obtained during the five months that I acted as receiver. Throughout this period, I regularly recorded impressions from the mind of Wilkins, three nights each week, from 11:30 to 12 midnight, New York Eastern Standard Time, Wilkins adjusting the difference in time at his end, as he flew farther north.

The results, when later checked against Wilkins' diary and log, after my impressions had been mailed, each night, to Dr. Gardner Murphy at Columbia University, for observation and filing, were far above chance. The complete account of these tests, with affidavits of witnesses and documentary evidence is contained in the book, "Thoughts Through Space," written in collaboration with Sir Hubert Wilkins. What I wish to emphasize here are a few of the discoveries we made about the functioning of mind, which have a direct bearing upon the operation of your own consciousness.

They can be summarized as follows:

1. It had been planned that Wilkins would get off by himself each appointed time and relive and review in his mind's eye the outstanding things that had happened to his research expedition or himself that day, while I, in New York, would sit quietly at the desk in my study, with my mind receptive, and attempt to record in words what I "saw" or "felt" in my own consciousness. As these experiments progressed, however, there were occasions when Wilkins was unable to keep the appointments but, to our surprise, the accuracy of my impressions remained undiminished.

This caused Wilkins to feel that, if he knew in advance that he could not put his thought upon me, at the given time, he could transmit them to me at spare moments during the day and he was then confident, when the regular time came for reception of these thoughts, I would find them waiting in my subconscious, ready to come through.

Certainly the results seemed to indicate that there was some substance to Wilkins' conviction because the reception appeared almost as good either way. I felt somewhat like a telegrapher who, upon opening his key, finds a number of messages on file. They would crowd through from my Subconscious, usually in the order of their feeling intensity, with the strongest thoughts catching my attention first.

2. This fact led to another discovery which we came to regard as axiomatic. The experiences which affected Wilkins the deepest, emotionally, were the ones I usually received the clearest and

easiest. This indicated that each thought has a definite relationship to feeling and that the more intense the feeling, the more powerful the thought.

In my opinion, this is one of the most profoundly significant facts that can ever be learned about the operation of mind. It explains why tragic events are sensed by humans many more times than those experiences which arouse little or no intensity of feeling.

Emotions must then be regarded as the generators of power behind thought, and the axiom can thus be stated:

The degree of intensity of emotional reaction to anything that happens to you, determines the degree of intensity of the thought wave discharged.

Drop a pebble into a pool of water and it scarcely makes a ripple. Toss in a large rock and you produce violent waves which extend in all directions. But thought, which exists in an electromagnetic field, once discharged from individual consciousness, is instantaneously receivable wherever there may be another individual consciousness, a part of this same field, attuned to it. The chances of reception will be increased in direct proportion to the intensity of the thought which has been discharged.

3. This being true, another fact or law of mind became obvious. I discovered that I could reach out, with my mind, into what we regard as time and space, by focalizing and intensifying my own emotional desires, to secure certain knowledge or to make contact with the thoughts of Wilkins. In this case, I was not dependent upon the power generated by Wilkins but was operating on my own consciously energized power. The question is now raised—did I project or extend my awareness to the physical area where Wilkins was and return with impressions received, not only from his mind, but from things and minds associated with him?

If I did, then the generation of my own power, through an intensified desire to receive, enabled me, at times, to pick up thought vibrations from minds and things which were too weak to be received otherwise. This can be likened to a powerful radio receiving set, so sensitized that it brings in the programs of weak broadcasting stations, which less powerful receiving sets could not even detect.

4. It became apparent, as our experiments continued, that more than what is generally recognized as telepathy was occurring. Impressions came to me of thoughts and conditions which were entirely unknown to Wilkins at the time. I had pre-visions of two accidents which were to befall his plane a week to ten days in advance of their happening and sensed, in my mind, that these mishaps had not yet taken place.

In the one, I described the trouble I "foresaw" developing in the crankcase and, in the other, I reported the plane taking off with a heavy load of gasoline and compelled to make a landing, due to a severe snowstorm, which resulted in the tail skid being torn away.

Wilkins subsequently confirmed these two precognitive impressions, testifying in the first instance, that a bearing had suddenly been ground to powder in the crankcase just before take-off and, in the second instance, that his plane, carrying a heavy load of gasoline on an attempted long search flight, was forced down when it encountered a blinding snowstorm, landing on the frozen bed of a river with such force that the tail skid was torn off. This ability of the mind to foresee the future led me to these conclusions:

A—The causes which were to produce these effects in some future moment of time must have existed in the present. For example, the bearing in the crankcase was no doubt worn and defective. While Wilkins nor any member of his crew knew this, my mind, in some unexplainable manner, must have sensed it, perhaps from the intelligence of the very particles themselves, because everything radiates *what it is,* at any given moment.

My mind, under direction to determine what was happening to Wilkins, had, in this case, focalized upon its detection that something was going to go wrong in the crankcase, which would lead to an event, in time, that would have an effect not only upon the mechanics of the plane but the consciousness of the humans involved.

To sense this development, the mind had to possess the capacity to see the chain of causes and effects which would ultimately eventuate in the burning out of the bearing. This illustrates how many happenings are in the process of externalizing themselves in the lives of all humans, in future moments of time, without these humans possessing any conscious knowledge of their approach.

B—As to the second instance, when the plane was forced down in the snowstorm and the tail skid was torn off, the cause of this accident was obviously the bad weather which arose at the time. Today, weather bureaus possess the technical know-how to make long range forecasts of fair and stormy weather for a month or more in advance, based upon existing present conditions. It therefore becomes partially understandable, at least, how my mind, starting with a current weather condition, followed through with the various repercussions of one weather change upon another and arrived at a point in future time where Wilkins and his plane, if they took off at such a time, would become involved in an accident of sufficient violence to bring about the previously described result.

But why and how I should sense the tail skid as the specific part of the plane which would be damaged, remains a mystery to me. Apparently these extra sensory powers function with great accuracy and precision but considerable of this accuracy may be lost in transmission from the Subconscious to the Conscious. This is because the Conscious mind, in its natural dependence upon the five physical senses, tends to discount and even reject extra sensory impressions or, if they are too strong to be turned aside, often permits these impressions to be colored by imagination and by previously acquired knowledge in order to make them appear more plausible to reason.

This tendency is one of the most difficult to guard against for anyone who attempts to act as receiver in the transmission of thought. Eventually, with practice, one can recognize an extra sensory impression when it strikes consciousness and, through an act of will, hold the imagination and other functions of mind in check. This distinction between a super normal and a normal thought is one of *feeling*.

C—The fact that the mind can sometimes foresee the future does not imply predestination. It is true that these two accidents occurred as envisioned, but this simply means, in my opinion, that the causative forces behind these two possible mishaps were not altered from the moment that my mind sensed them until the time of their materialization. But, if the plane mechanic had discovered the defect in the bearing of the crankcase at any time after my receipt of the impression, up to a few moments before the actual happening, he could have averted the accident by removal of this bearing. Similarly, if the time of the flight had been changed so that it no longer coincided with the sudden outbreak of the storm, no forced landing would have been necessary and the tail skid would not have been torn off the plane. Thus it can be seen that the type of precognitive impressions which your mind might receive in any one moment of time could be entirely altered in the very next moment of time IF the causative elements with which your mind is in touch, should have been removed or changed.

5. There is evidence that once two individuals have become closely associated by marriage, business or friendship, some sort of magnetic affinity is established between their minds. Many have discovered that they often seem to think and feel alike. They usually ascribe this, not to extra sensory perception, but to an acquired familiarity with each other's thoughts and habits. It is my conviction that the stronger thoughts and feelings two people have for one another, the more apt they are to sense each other's moods, inclinations, thoughts and acts. This magnetic attraction continues to exist throughout life, whether the individuals remain together or stray apart. This accounts for the innumerable cases wherein a man or woman, after long separation from a friend or loved one, may receive an inexplicable feeling of his nearness,

illness or death. That these impressions are later proved to be true confirms the fact that the minds of each have remained subconsciously attuned and the intense feeling of one has been communicated to the other.

I can best illustrate this phenomenon by reciting several experiences in relation to Wilkins. Some years after our experiments, when I was living in Chicago, Sir Hubert had his headquarters in Washington, D.C. going and coming from this point in the research work he was doing for the United States Army. We kept in touch by correspondence, exchanging letters every month or so. Invariably, as I would fix my mind upon Wilkins, while writing him, a vivid impression would hit me.

On one occasion, I was impelled to add a postscript, stating: "It seems to me you have just had a narrow escape of some kind. I see you surrounded by clouds of smoke and fire. You appear to be coughing and choking. I cannot understand this feeling."

Some ten days later, when Wilkins had returned to Washington from a trip and found my letter awaiting, he answered: "How odd that you should have received such an impression! On that date, I tested a new asbestos suit for the United States Army. Five hundred gallons of high test gas were touched off and I was required to walk through the flames. The asbestos suit sprang a leak and I was almost suffocated before they could get me out."

At another time, in the act of writing a letter to Wilkins, the impression came to me that he had recently injured his arm and shoulder. I so stated and inquired if he had been in an accident of some kind. Wilkins wrote that he had indeed been in an accident. He was in a bus returning to Washington when, a few miles out from the city, the bus veered to avoid collision with another car near a bridge, rolled down an embankment and overturned in the river. Wilkins escaped through a window, breaking his collar bone and injuring his arm. Three people were drowned, including an elderly lady to whom Wilkins had given his seat in the front of the bus behind the driver.

At still another time, when writing Wilkins, I had the feeling that he had injured his chest in some way. I reported this impression to him and he replied that the past weekend he had visited his farm in Pennsylvania and, while carrying a watermelon to the house, had tripped and fallen, landing on the melon and cracking several ribs.

It is to be noted that the incidents I sensed, with my mind attuned to Wilkins, were each highly emotional in nature and their very intensity aided my reception.

6. In the receiving of thought impressions, I found that the *first* impressions which flashed, unbidden and without any possible association, into consciousness, were usually correct. If I recognized and accepted them instantly, I was able to hold them long enough to interpret their meaning and record them. But if I wavered in my reception long enough to permit my imagination and my logic to become active, the impression would either be rejected as having no basis in fact or so altered as to be worthless.

One must develop sufficient discipline of mind to discriminate between genuine extra sensory impressions and simulated ones created by wishful thinking or feelings of fear and apprehension.

In this connection, the less you know concerning a place, a thing or a person, the more certain you can be that the impressions you receive about them are correct. The normal functions of mind endeavor to aid you by contributing, if permitted, such information as you have already naturally acquired in the course of your life and association relative to this place, thing or person. Such information, obtained through the five physical senses, instead of proving helpful, will always color and distort a genuine extra sensory impression which may be at complete variance to all previously known facts.

In all of the years I have devoted to the study of these higher powers of mind, my fundamental interest and purpose has been to determine the ways in which these powers might be harnessed and applied for practical, beneficial use in everyday life. This, I feel sure, will represent your own interest.

To attain any satisfying development of the extra sensory faculties in your own mind, you must first be convinced that they actually do exist. So long as you maintain a strong attitude of doubt, the force of your very skepticism and disbelief inhibits these powers from manifesting.

I discovered early in my experimentation that it was necessary for me to assume, on faith, that these higher senses not only existed but would operate for me under proper direction, before I could obtain any positive results. To the degree that I could develop a confident, expectant state of receptivity, ruling out doubt and apprehension, just to that degree would these extra sensory faculties respond with verifiable impressions. Once you establish in consciousness the conviction that you possess these higher powers, and the expectation and desire that they will function with increasing facility in your life, you will be rewarded by a steadily expanding inner consciousness.

Scientists and researchers have thus far been baffled by the varied nature of super normal phenomena, being at a loss as to how to classify it. For purposes of your own study, it will be helpful to you to regard your intuition as the faculty through which any and all of these varied phenomena of Extra Sensory Perception may manifest.

Actually, you will soon make the discovery that your extra sensory faculties have been serving you all your life, so subtly blending with your five physical senses that you have seldom recognized their operation. You can reflect now upon many strong, intuitional urges you have had, to do or not to do a certain thing, which did not have their origin in your conscious mind or in any existing knowledge of conditions about you. You have had feelings for or against people upon first meeting or during association which could not be explained on the basis of any testimony of your five physical senses. You can perhaps recall premonitions of an impending event which you may or may not have followed, to your loss or gain. It is even possible you have had a fleeting vision of some loved one or friend in trouble, ill, injured or dying, or that you have seen such events in a dream. These and many other kinds of phenomena have been at the door of consciousness and, at times, have pushed this door slightly ajar, pressing for conscious recognition.

Through meditation, as previously stated, you can activate your extra sensory powers to work for you. When you pray, at the same time visualizing what you desire, you are in effect telling the Creative Power within, with which your extra sensory faculties are associated, to help attract what you need to you, as an answer to this prayer.

Suggestion is a powerful motivator of mind. Make clear to these inner powers what you really want. Exercise sufficient faith that your prayers will be answered and the God Power within will speak to you through your intuition, offering guidance in the form of what you may have called hunches, urges, premonitions, dreams, visions and the like which, if properly interpreted and acted upon, prove material aids to the answer of prayer.

Once you have learned how to project consciously a picture upon the inner mind, accompanied by a prayerful desire for its materialization, it will not be necessary for you to confine these visualizing moments to the meditation periods alone, but you will be able to employ them at different times of the day or night, wherever you may be and whenever you feel the need. With practice, the technique of meditation will have become subconscious and when you have accomplished conscious attunement with the God Consciousness within, you will be able to reach this Consciousness at will, to convey your specific need and to start creative forces at work within you in fulfillment of that need.

Upon reaching this point in your development you become, to quite a degree, the conscious creator of your own destiny. Since the Subconscious part of you is not limited by time or space, the more you draw upon these extra sensory faculties, the less limited you become in your dealings with time and space. You will discover many ways in which you may instruct your higher powers to serve you, and one of these effective ways will be what I call "synchronizing your movements in time." This involves your mental ability to make time work for you. By so doing, you can always be at the right place at the right time and accomplish what you desire in and through time. I have used this method of thinking for so many years that it has now become second nature with me.

On a trip to New York City some time ago, Mrs. Sherman and I read in the papers that DeMille's new picture, "Greatest Show on Earth" had just opened at Radio City Music Hall, and that all reserved seats were sold out for weeks, with general admission crowds standing in line for blocks. Because I had always retained a small boy's love of circuses, I had an especial desire to see this picture but we were to have little time free during our short stay in the city to see any show. Checking in at the hotel in late afternoon, I left Mrs. Sherman to unpack and hurried down to the old barber shop on Forty-fourth Street, near Fifth Avenue, where I had been served some years before while living in New York.

I found some of the barbers still there and they told me that the head man, whom I also knew, was out but would be back any time. As I was relaxing in the barber chair, eyes closed, having a facial massage, my thoughts centered upon the show at the Music Hall. It occurred to me that this first night in New York might be our best time to see the picture if I could get tickets to the reserved section.

I saw myself, in my mind's eye, stepping up to the reservations window, despite the presence of a "Sold Out" sign, and getting two seats. As soon as this impression hit me, I recognized it as a flash of inner awareness and I felt that, if I co-operated properly with this urge, these tickets would be made available. I left the barber chair long enough to phone Mrs. Sherman at the hotel and ask her if she felt like going to the picture should we be able to get in. She said she did, and I returned to the barber chair, spending the remaining time in it quietly and confidently visualizing myself in possession of the desired tickets.

When the barber was finished, and I was ready to leave, anxious to get to the theatre, I was delayed by the arrival of the head barber who greeted me as an old friend and kept me talking to him for some twenty minutes. By the time I reached the Music Hall at Fiftieth and Sixth Avenue, it was shortly after 6 P.M. and there was a tremendous crowd about the entrance and jamming the sidewalk toward Fifth Avenue, as far as the eye could see. The doorman behind the ropes kept repeating: "Sorry . . . all sold out! Sorry . . . all sold out!" in an effort to keep the crowd moving. He turned back the attempts of any who tried to get beyond the ropes and into the theatre lobby.

To all external appearances, there was not the remotest chance of getting in to see the show unless one took his place in the line and waited several hours to do so, which Mrs. Sherman and I were not inclined to do because of our long motor trip that day.

I approached the doorman and said: "I'm from out of town, and I'd like to get reserved seats for any performance I can. Will you please let me through to the reserved seat window?" He said, "Okay" and lifted the rope. I now hurried in to the inner lobby and encountered a vacuum around the reservations windows. There was the "Sold Out" sign, as I had foreseen. I stopped short, on impulse, and took stock of the situation. I could hear the girls in the two windows answering telephone calls from ticket agencies and individuals, saying over and over: "No— nothing for tonight . . . sold out for five weeks .. . nothing for tonight . . ."

It sounded hopeless but the picture still persisted in my mind that I was going to one of the windows and get two tickets. At the moment, however, I felt impelled to hold back the while I tried to determine just what my approach might be in asking for admissions. I had the hope that there might be some "house seats" left which the management often retains till the last minute for visiting celebrities or other special demands. It occurred to me that I might tell the box office girl that I had formerly lived in New York and had attended the original opening night at the Music Hall and had been a regular patron for some time, hoping that this true personal appeal would cause her to release any tickets which might be cached away.

But, while I was standing by, still uncertain as to the next move, the answer to my compelling desire materialized in the form of a man who entered from the lobby with three tickets in his hand. He hurried to the window and I instinctively stepped in behind him.

"I'm sorry," I heard him say to the box office girl, "my mother has been taken ill and my wife and I can't go to the show tonight. Can I turn these in for a later date?" The girl made the exchange and, as the man left the window, I stepped up. The girl in the booth adjoining reached for the phone and said: "How many did you get? I've got a place for them."

"Just a minute!" I heard myself saying to the box office girl in front of me, and then I repeated what I had visualized myself telling her, ending with the plea, "So, for old time's sake, would you give me a break and let me have two of those three tickets, please?"

The girl smiled and tossed out the tickets. "You win, Mister," she said. Then to the girl on the phone, "Tell him all you've got left is a *single*."

An analysis of this experience will prove revealing. From the moment in the barber shop that I intuitively felt it would be possible for me to get reserved seats that night for the show, it was only necessary that I let myself continue to be guided by my extra sensory perceptions for this desire to be realized.

Consciously, I was eager to get to the theatre as soon as I left the barber chair, but I was detained some twenty minutes in conversation with the head barber. As later developments demonstrated, this delay was absolutely necessary as, otherwise, I would have arrived at the box office window before this man returned his tickets, and would have left empty-handed. Even so, had I not been impulsed to delay my approach to the window, standing by for perhaps five minutes, I would still have been turned down and would have gone from the window entirely unaware that, within a few minutes following my departure, the tickets I might have had were available.

Consider, from this, what split second and sensitized synchronizing of time between my movements and the movements of all concerned was necessary to the fulfillment of my desire! How these extra sensory faculties can contact all conditions and peoples associated with any specific objective and correlate all actions leading up to the moment of achievement or realization is a profound mystery. But there is abundant evidence to indicate that these higher powers of mind do just this, time and time and time again, and we, blindly, ascribe it all to chance or luck or coincidence.

Mark Twain recognized the existence of these higher powers in telling of an experience of his own. He said he had need of an article, some years later, that he had written for the Christian Herald in an 1885 issue. He wrote the publishers for it only to be advised that the demand for this particular issue had been so great they did not even have a file copy left. Twain's own file copy had gotten away from him. He was disturbed at this news and, more than ever determined to get a copy, began asking different friends if they chanced to have this issue among their effects. None happened to have it and his inability to secure a copy was holding up some current writing he intended to undertake with reference to this article. Twain felt there must be someone, somewhere, who had the publication and he ardently wished he might run into such a person.

Several weeks later, while in New York City on business from his home in Hartford, Connecticut, Mark Twain was stopped by traffic at Fifth Avenue and Forty-second Street. While he was standing there, awaiting his opportunity to cross, a strange man, one of hundreds who had been passing, suddenly stopped upon recognizing the famous author, and addressed him: "Oh, Mr. Twain! This is odd! I was just on my way to the office to mail you this old magazine. I was cleaning out my files last night and came across it. I found it contained an article you had written and since it was published some years ago, it occurred to me you might like to have it."

With this, the man handed an envelope to Twain who thanked him and the stranger then disappeared in the stream of passers-by. Twain opened the envelope and discovered, to his amazement, that it contained the very copy of the Christian Herald which he had been seeking.

In commenting upon this remarkable "coincidence," Twain wondered at the circumstances which had caused him to be halted by traffic at that particular corner at the specific time that this man should be passing. He marveled even more at the mysterious force or intelligence which had moved this man to go through his files and, upon coming across the copy of the Christian Herald, to get the urge to send it to Twain.

Such an occurrence, and many like it, are still mysteries today. We cannot explain the process by which these extra sensory powers, in response to our desires, so influence our physical movements and mental decisions as to bring all needed factors together at some point in time and place. In Twain's case, the operation of his extra sensory powers was so effective that, had they failed to bring him in contact with the stranger on the street, this man's consciousness had been so impressed with the urgency of getting this magazine to Twain, that he would have mailed it and Twain would have received it anyway!

This is additional evidence that we all exist in the Great Subconscious, through a vast network of interrelated, individualized subconscious minds. Mark Twain had only to send out the call for this copy of the Christian Herald with sufficient emotionalized force behind it to reach its objective in the mind of a man in whose subconscious mind resided the knowledge that he had the magazine in his possession. The urge then came to this man, impelled by the influence of Twain's thought, to clean out his files, which seemed to have been a natural inclination. The moment, however, that he got his hands on the Christian Herald, he was impulsed to focalize his attention upon it, and when he saw the Mark Twain article in it, the full impact of Twain's projected need, in thought form, hit him. He reacted to it with what he felt was a thought of his own, that Twain might have use for this article, and he would mail it to him the following day, upon arrival at his office. Actually, this man had responded perfectly, both consciously and subconsciously to Twain's mental broadcast, and had synchronized his movements in time and space with Twain's.

The uses to which you can put your extra sensory powers, once recognized and developed, are many and varied. You can actually train your mind to protect you from loss or injury, if you properly direct it.

Some years ago, while living in New York City, Charles Forbell, well known cartoonist, and his wife, came to visit us one evening. When they left our apartment around midnight, they found that a burglar had jimmied open the door of their car and stolen a new suit of clothes that Mr. Forbell had purchased that day. We naturally felt badly at this loss and, in meditation that night, reflecting upon this experience, I charged my mind with the following thought: "No one can try to steal anything of mine without my being made aware of it in time to prevent the theft." I repeated this thought in consciousness, with deep feeling and authority. When I felt my inner mind had been sufficiently impressed with this command, I turned my thought to other meditative matters.

There is an old saying that "an elephant never forgets." You may be sure that your subconscious never forgets. Not limited by time or space, every mental order given to it exists in the NOW.

More than two years passed, and I was then serving as editor of the Savings Bank Journal, with offices on east Forty-second Street. Milton Harrison, the publisher, asked me late one afternoon to stay downtown and have dinner with him so we could discuss editorial problems. I slipped on my winter overcoat and walked with him to the elevator. Then, on sudden impulse, I had him hold the elevator while I returned to my office, picked up a copy of the latest issue of the Savings Bank Journal, folded it and put it in my inside overcoat pocket. Why I felt the need for that extra copy I couldn't explain since I had taken my two regular file copies home with me several days before, and I did not require this publication for our conference.

We went to dine at Stouffer's Restaurant, on the ground floor of a nearby building, a place where we had eaten many times. I hung my coat on a rack some fifty feet from the table at which we were seated. During the course of the meal, scores of men and women came and went, making use of this same coat rack. I hadn't given my coat the slightest thought when, suddenly, in the midst of conversation with Mr. Harrison, a strong intuitive feeling hit me as though an inner voice was saying: "That man is walking out with your overcoat!"

Having trained myself to follow my hunches, I rose from the table and started toward the cashier's desk where a man, just buttoning up an overcoat, was waiting to pay his check. My coat was a plain black coat, similar to hundreds of others, with no external distinguishing marks. But the impact of this feeling that the man on his way out was wearing my coat was so strong that I hurried up to him and grabbed his arm. At this instant, my conscious mind began to react to the situation and to argue against my impression by saying: "You'd better be careful. If this man doesn't have your coat, you can get in trouble!"

But I had gone this far and something impelled me to go further. "I beg your pardon," I said, "but I believe you have my coat!"

The man glared at me and tried to pull away. "Oh, no, I don't! Let go of me!"

The coat was fully buttoned. I had no way of proving that it was really mine and I was about to release him when another intuitive message struck me. "If this is your coat, it has your Savings Bank Journal in the inside pocket."

Instinctively, I reached for the top button, jerked open the coat, and there, surely enough, was the magazine. "You *do* have my coat," I insisted. "Take it off!"

The man's attitude instantly changed. "I'm sorry, sir —very sorry! I'd have sworn . . . that looked just like my . . . Here you are . . ." He handed me the coat and started back toward the coat rack as though to get his own coat, then suddenly made a break and dashed out the front door.

The manager of Stouffer's, who knew me, came rushing up with the excited query: "Mr. Sherman, did that man try to steal your coat?"

"Yes," I said, "I guess he did."

The manager shook his head, in disappointment. "I wish you'd held him," he said. "We've had six overcoats stolen here in the past week, and we've been trying to catch the thief."

Several days later I had lunch at Stouffer's and found a little folder beside my plate, which had apparently been printed following my episode. On the front cover were the words:

Your

HAT and

COAT

Inside, was the picture of a man walking out of the restaurant with his hat and coat on. In the space opposite, the warning:

. . . about your hat and coat

Unfortunately, not everyone is honest . . . and wherever people gather nowadays for entertainment or eating . . . there are those who seize such an opportunity to steal.

Such thefts do occasionally occur . . . so let us caution you to watch your hat and coat.

It is manifestly impossible for us to do so, or be responsible for such losses.

Apparently, I hadn't needed to watch my coat. My mind had done the watching for me. As I analyzed this occurrence, it was plain to me that my mind was following a suggestion given to it two years before when I had commanded, in that period of meditation: "No one can try to steal anything of mine without my being made aware of it in time to prevent the theft." Not only that, but my extra sensory faculties must have had an awareness of this attempted theft which was coming toward me in time, and could foresee that I was going to need something in the coat by which I could identify it, and so gave me the impulse to return to my office and place a copy of the Savings Bank Journal in the pocket. Then, when the man started out with my overcoat, I was made consciously aware of his action and given such a strong conviction that I unhesitatingly approached and challenged him At the critical moment when he defied me, my inner mind supplied me with the support I needed to back up my accusation. I thought of the Savings Bank Journal and located it in the pocket.

The timing of this entire extra sensory process and the steps it took to protect me were little short of amazing, but now I have long since learned to accept such operations of these higher powers of mind as the work of the God Consciousness within me in answer to desires expressed through meditation and prayer.

It should be observed that I have had to act in response to the intuitive feelings on impulses I have received. Had I refused to recognize them or had I sought to establish their logic in the light of surface appearances, these higher powers could not have served me. Nor can they serve any person who is not attuned and alert to their functioning. Incidentally, it may be of interest to know that this is the only time in my life that anyone has attempted to steal anything from me so there was no existing apprehension in my mind of a possible robbery.

Living in New York City for so many years and doing much traveling by taxi cab, I was frequently impressed with the recklessness of drivers and the great number of bad accidents. I decided, one night, during my period of meditation, that I needed to provide mental protection against any possible accident in which I might become involved. I therefore pictured myself being warned by the God Power within me in advance of such an accident and doing instinctively the right thing in an emergency. I had unquestioned faith that my extra sensory faculties would follow my instruction and see me safely through any moment of danger. Having thus pictured receiving necessary guidance and protection, I went about my daily activities and my travels free of all fears and apprehensions, in the relaxed assurance that all would be well.

Some weeks later, I was in a hurry to get downtown for a business appointment. I hailed a cab and seated myself on the left behind the driver. I had spent long hours at the typewriter that day and I was enjoying this chance to relax on the ride across town. All of a sudden, as the driver was passing through 128th Street, approaching Fifth Avenue, a feeling of great uneasiness swept over me. I was alerted at once and impelled to move from the left or uptown side of the cab, to the far right. This had no sooner been done than my driver, absent-mindedly, started across Fifth Avenue against the lights and in the face of onrushing traffic.

I saw in a glance that we were going to be hit broadside by an old sedan, which was later found to have been loaded with heavy iron pipe. My first inclination was to grab the strap beside the car door and cling to it, but as I did so, an inner voice seemed to say, "Let go of that and cover up!"

Responding to this intuitive flash, I put my arms over my face and head and pulled up my legs, knees close to the chest, to protect the vital parts of my body. At this moment, we were struck with such force the cab was turned over in mid-air, landed on the roof, rolled over twice, wheels torn off, and came to rest against a lamp post on the far side of Fifth Avenue, shattering it with the impact. During this time, I was as loose in the body of the cab as a rubber ball. Glass from the breaking windows was showering about me and I twice recall being on my back on the inside roof of the cab looking up between my arms at the floor of the car above me. When the battered cab finally stopping rolling, it was lying on its side and I was on my back, knees and arms still protecting body and head. The rear seat cushion and one of the spare seats on top of me.

A quick inventory determined that my right arm appeared to be dislocated at the elbow and there was a bump on my head, otherwise I seemed perfectly all right. Pushing the seat cushion off me, I saw that the left side of the cab where I had been sitting was all bashed in, and the door jammed off its hinges. A voice outside cried: "Look out for fire! Is anyone in there?"

Then a powerfully built man clambered up, straddled the door and looked down at me. He asked how badly I was hurt and if I could get up. When I assured him I could, he said: "Hurry up, Mister. This cab's apt to blow any minute." As I got to my feet with some difficulty, my rescuer grasped the door and wrenched it loose from the car. Then he reached down, placed his hands under my armpits and dragged me out. Traffic was stopped in both directions, police cars were just arriving, a crowd of several hundred had gathered and my driver, who was seated on the curb, moaning, was nursing a broken collar bone. My last sight of him had been his letting go the wheel and diving to the floor of his cab at the moment of the crash. The car did not catch fire.

When I was safely home, having stopped at my doctor's to have the light arm and head injuries attended, I did much reflecting on the accident. I recalled the precision with which my extra sensory faculties had taken charge in obeyance to the protective pattern I had placed in consciousness some weeks before. My mind had warned in advance of the accident, not only that it was about to occur but that my position on the left side of the cab was extremely hazardous. I had been given the compelling impulse to move as far as I could to the right and then to protect my body with arms and legs. The wisdom of my letting go the strap was emphasized by the insurance adjustor who called the next day and who told me that their case histories of other accidents, much less severe than this one had been, revealed that men and women who had clung to the straps had taken such a battering that it had resulted in serious head and body injuries or death. He said to me: "Grabbing that strap is the most natural thing for any human to do. Why didn't you do it?"

There wasn't any understandable explanation for me to offer him except to say that it had seemed like a better idea to do what I had done. My body had tossed around in the cab amid showers of glass, seat cushions, one of the spare seats and other objects but because they, too, were all in motion, none struck me too hard and I emerged from what could easily have been a fatal crash, practically unharmed.

This experience, quite naturally, increased my faith in the infallible protective nature of the God Power within when properly directed. I repeated my meditation with even greater conviction for several nights, thanking God for the guidance and care I had received.

* * *

Several years later, to prove that this was not just a remarkable happenstance, I was en route down Broadway in another cab when the motor suddenly began to cough and miss. This, in itself, is seldom cause for alarm. Any regular rider of cabs has heard many car engines act up in his time. But, on this occasion, I was seized with a feeling of intense apprehension. I said to the driver, "If you're going to have trouble, let me out so I can catch another cab. I'm in a hurry."

But the driver, anxious to keep his fare, replied: "Aw—it'll be all right, Mister. It's been actin' this way all morning."

As he spoke, the motor *did* clear up and the engine functioned all right for a block or so. My conscious mind began its usual argument with me. There wasn't any need for me to have been disturbed. This was a false alarm. I leaned back, wondering why such a feeling had come to me if there had been no real extra sensory basis for it, when the motor once more commenced to miss. We were approaching 137th Street and there were empty cabs parked along the curb. A feeling of the greatest urgency hit me and a voice seemed to say: "Get out of this cab! Get out, *quick!*"

The driver was fussing with the accelerator, and I shouted to him "Pull over to the curb! I'm getting out!"

He protested but I insisted. As he pulled over, I got the door open and was just getting out when there was an explosion and the cab went up in flames. The driver jumped out on his side and we stood, watching the car consumed. The fire department was there in a few minutes but the cab was soon a blackened ruin. I continued my trip downtown in another cab.

Once again I had been saved from possible serious injury or death by the impelling action of the God Power within. One can testify most authoritatively of those experiences which have come to him For this reason, although I could cite many of such similar incidents of protection accorded me during my life, I wish to narrate only one more, as conclusive evidence that these occurrences have nothing whatsoever to do with chance or the functioning of the five physical senses alone. I would like you to clearly see how the higher powers of mind fuse their operations with your ordinary senses in order to accomplish a result in your external life.

In Arkansas, several years ago, I was returning from Little Rock in my Buick sedan which was carrying five neighbor men from the hill country adjoining our farm. We had been to the city to appear before the Public Service Commission in presenting a petition to secure rural electrification. This committee of men with me were all fathers and responsible citizens of their community.

A few miles outside of Beebe, on paved highway 67, I was trailing a light blue truck by a little over a hundred feet. It, in turn, was trailing a red truck ahead of it. My speed was around fifty miles per hour and the blue truck was apparently making the same speed because it had maintained its position ahead of me for the past several miles. The red truck was only making thirty-five miles per hour and this partially accounted for what happened.

Suddenly, with absolutely no warning, the driver of the blue truck slammed on all brakes, foot pedal and emergency. This locked his wheels and the truck almost jumped off the pavement, turning sidewise and blocking both lanes of the highway. I had a hundred feet or less to avoid hitting it. Instantly, something in my consciousness took over. It was a time for split-second decisions, when things were destined to happen so fast in the next fractions of seconds that the conscious mind, alone, could not cope with them.

A quick glance revealed to me that there was a soft, narrow shoulder and a ditch beyond filled with water, and beyond that, a rock embankment. Ahead of me, perhaps seventy-five feet, was a solid concrete post supporting a road side. There wasn't sufficient space between it and the tail end of the blue truck for me to go between. Pressing hard on the foot brake to reduce my speed, I sideswiped this post, shearing it off and taking my right fender with it. I missed the end of the stalled truck by a hair on the opposite side and then, as I ran off on the shoulder, I spun the steering wheel to the left and hit the accelerator. The left front wheel stayed on the highway and the rear of the car swung around on the soft shoulder.

I was now clear of the blue truck but found the red truck also stopped and dead ahead of me. The driver of this truck, an elderly man, having seen through his rear view mirror that the blue truck was about to hit him, had become paralyzed with fright and, instead of stepping on the gas and getting out of the danger zone, had set his own brakes.

Instinctively reacting to this second danger, I kept whipping the steering wheel to the left, alternately pressing my foot against the brake pedal, then the accelerator, and barely knifed past the end of the red truck off onto the left shoulder of the road. I was now faced with the peril of going off into the ditch on that side.

How I physically managed to brake the car and spin the steering wheel hard right and then give the car sufficient gas to cause it to pull out, around and ahead of this red truck, I will never know. My Buick must have been on two wheels part of this time, and for the next two hundred yards, I snaked down the highway, first in one lane and then in the other, fighting to bring the car under complete control. As I did so, two cars going at least sixty miles an hour passed me in their own lanes. Their drivers had seen the accident and my frantic maneuvers, but had been going too fast themselves to stop and, in much less time than it has taken to tell this, I had gone around and between the light blue and the red track and straightened out on my side of the road, in the split second necessary to avoid a head-on collision with the approaching cars!

The moment I could manage to stop, I jumped out of the car and ran back up the highway to see what had caused the driver of the light blue truck to jam on his brakes as he had, without warning, thus precipitating this narrowest of escapes from a terrible highway tragedy. I saw that this driver, since I had passed him, had put his truck in reverse, had backed completely off the highway, and that the rear of the truck was in the ditch, half-submerged in water.

As I reached the truck, the driver staggered out, bleary-eyed, and fell flat on his face, dead drunk. I needed no explanation after that. He had obviously been no gauge of distance in his condition and had come up on the slower moving vehicle too fast. Realizing, at the last moment, he was about to hit it, he turned to the left to go around it and jammed on his brakes so hard that all wheels locked, leaving his truck sidewise of the highway, across both lanes.

When I returned to my own car and the silent group of men who had made not a move or a sound throughout those few awful seconds, Mr. Noricks, who had sat in the front seat beside me, remarked: "Mr. Sherman—I'd have talked to God if I'd had time!"

I didn't say anything but I knew that God had talked to me through my extra sensory faculties, and that He had said just the right thing to do to cause me to make the right moves to bring me and my fellow passengers safely through the most harrowing traffic experience of my life.

Sometimes your intuition will bring you flashes of the future concerning yourself or others. I had an amusing illustration of this when I was in Portland on lecture tour and met Emma Smiley, leader of a New Thought group in Victoria, B.C. I asked her if she was going to attend the INTA convention which was to be held in Chicago in mid-July. She said that her daughter was expecting a baby girl about that time and that she could not take in the convention for that reason.

As she said this, my mind suddenly brought me the impression that the new arrival would be delayed for several weeks and that when it finally came, it would be a boy. I told Mrs. Smiley that she would have *plenty* of time to go to the Chicago convention and return before her daughter presented her with a *grandson*. She said: "You awful man—I already have a grandson. Don't tell me I'm going to have another one! I want a little granddaughter this time."

I laughed and said I was sorry but all I could "see" was a *boy*.

On August 16th, I received the following note from Mrs. Smiley:

"Hi—I still don't like that man!

It was a boy! Arrived July 31st!

I'm sure it's all your fault. Why didn't you say it was a girl?

Sorry to be so late in letting you know—but Grandma is a very busy woman."

Years ago in New York, I took a position as editor of a trade publication with the Edward Lyman Bill Publishing Company, on Madison Avenue. I had not been at this editorial work long when an editor of one of the other magazines came through the offices selling chances at fifty cents apiece for two tickets in the sixth row center to "Rose Marie," one of the biggest musical comedy hits of all time. Scalpers were getting twenty-five dollars a pair for good seats even in those days. The editor explained that his wife's sudden illness prevented him from using these tickets for the following night, and that was why he was raffling them off. As he offered me a chance, the number "23" flashed to mind and I saw a fleeting mental picture of this number being drawn.

Reacting at once to this intuitive feeling, I said, "Do you have number twenty-three left? If you do, I'll buy it."

He laughed, looked through the numbers in his hand, and produced number "23." "Why do you want twenty-three?" he asked. "Is that your lucky number?"

"No," I replied, "but it's going to be today—because this is the number that's going to win!"

As a new man with this organization, the news spread through the offices that I had requested number "23" and had predicted that it would be the one chosen. When the drawing took place immediately after office hours, that afternoon, more than one hundred men and women good-naturedly assembled to witness the event, each holding his number. Edward Lyman Bill, the head of the publishing house, was asked to do the honors. He stood upon a desk, in sight of all, and the man who was raffling off the "Rose Marie" tickets dropped all the duplicate numbers in Mr. Bill's hat, shaking them up. Then, as he raised the hat for Mr. Bill to make the selection, he turned to me and said, "Well, Sherman, do you still think number '23' is going to win?"

"I certainly do!" I replied. "The rest of you folks might as well go home!"

There was a roar of laughter. Mr. Bill gave the numbers a big stir and then lifted one out. He glanced at it, unbelievingly, and stood, speechless for a moment.

"Tell us—what is it?" several cried out.

"Believe it or not," said Mr. Bill, "I swear to you this isn't a frame-up—but it's *twenty-three!*"

This sensing of the number that would be drawn was just a little thing but it was the talk of the office for many weeks to come. I could not have deliberated and determined what the Winning number would be but perhaps, in that instance, my desire to win those tickets because Mrs. Sherman and I could not afford to buy seats at that time, was so strong that it activated my extra sensory faculties to the point of projecting me ahead in time and giving me a glimpse of the number Mr. Bill would choose.

A somewhat similar experience came to me quite recently while lecturing in Glendale, California. I was invited to attend an afternoon luncheon meeting of the women's group of the Church of Religious Science. Tickets were being sold to be drawn for a prize. I was the only man present among more than a hundred women—in fact I was told that I was the first man to be invited to speak to this organization. When I was offered a chance to purchase a ticket, I said, jokingly, "You women don't want to sell any chances to me because, if you do, I'll win the prize—and I imagine the prize is for women only."

The women laughed and said they would be glad to take my money. "Okay," I told them, "I'll buy some chances on condition you let me pick out my own numbers."

I was handed the entire spool of canceled theatre tickets which were being used. Unwinding some yards of this spool, to their amusement, I tore off a little strip of tickets for myself at a point where I felt the impulse so to do. I then separated these few tickets and dropped them in the bowl with over a hundred others. When all tickets had been collected, the president of the women's club then took me by surprise as she turned and said: "Since Mr.,Sherman is so sure that he has picked out the winning ticket, we've decided to let him choose his own!"

With this, she held the bowl over my head. It was a humorously dramatic moment and I was, of course, on the spot. This had been started in fun but I had really tried to follow my intuition at the time the spool of tickets was in my hands. In my conscious mind I did not expect to be able to pick one of my own numbers but I thought I might as well try and see if I could get a feeling reaction to any particular ticket as it touched my hand. Taking a handful and letting them slip through my fingers, I was impulsed to hang onto one of them and let all the others go. I held it up and called off the number. No one had it. I looked at my duplicates. The number was mine. . . . The prize? A lady's apron!

This last case raises an interesting question. When I asked for the opportunity to select my own tickets, did I impart some vibration from me to them by contact and was I later able to sense this same vibration when I was challenged to choose my own ticket from the bowl?

If someone else had done the drawing would my number, in this instance, still have been picked out? It is difficult to tell.

There are always crises in one's life when one wishes he possessed a wisdom and an awareness far beyond the limitations of his five physical senses. It is seldom, however, due to our neglect in developing dependence upon the intuition, that we can safely call upon it under stress of difficult circumstances. Any attempt to force these extra sensory powers to bring you desperately needed information, insight or guidance only seems to wall off their functions entirely. It requires the establishment and maintenance of an inner poise, and quiet but expectant receptivity, for these powers to operate. This was profoundly impressed upon me in a grueling test to which I was subjected, shortly before Christmas of 1938.

Mrs. Sherman had been called to Michigan by the illness and subsequent death of her mother, leaving me at home in New York with our two daughters and Lelah, the colored maid. I was then employed as editor of the Savings Bank Journal. Bob Garland, bachelor friend, and then dramatic critic for the New York World-Telegram, phoned me at the office to say he was having a Christmas party in his Greenwich Village apartment for the children of married friends and he wanted to invite Marcia, our younger daughter, aged nine, to attend. Bob had a little Boston bull dog named "Telly" of which Marcia was fond. I knew she would enjoy going to such a party but I told Bob I had no way of getting her there with my working and Martha being out of town. Bob assured me that he could easily solve this problem since Mrs. Stern, who was bringing her daughter, would swing around and pick Marcia up in her car. In that case, I told Bob that Marcia could go and that when I finished work in late afternoon, I would come direct to his apartment and take her home.

That night I informed Marcia of Bob's invitation and told Lelah to have her ready to go with Mrs. Stern when she would call for Marcia around three-thirty P.M. the following afternoon. I then dismissed the subject from my mind as all arranged.

The next day was an extremely busy one for me, so busy that I was compelled to defer a luncheon appointment at the City Club on Forty-fourth Street until close to two o'clock. My mind was filled with business matters and it was not until about a quarter to four, when I was leaving the City Club to return to the office that I suddenly thought of Marcia. At this time she should have been on her way to Bob's in Mrs. Stern's car. But the instant I fixed my mind upon her, I was seized with a feeling of great uneasiness. I knew that something had gone wrong, the plans had been changed, Mrs. Stern was not calling for her after all. I stepped into the nearest telephone booth and phoned home.

"Lelah," I asked, when she came on the wire, "Mrs. Stern hasn't called for Marcia, has she?"

"No, Mr. Sherman," Lelah replied, "but everything's all right. Mr. Garland called and said Mrs. Stern couldn't get the car but to put Marcia on the Number Four Fifth Avenue bus—and he'd meet her at the end of the line."

"Lelah!" I said, "you didn't let her go!"

"Why, yes, Mr. Sherman," said Lelah. "I hope I didn't do anything wrong."

"I'm sure you didn't mean to," I replied, "but where did Mr. Garland tell Marcia to get off?"

"Oh, he told her not to get off. She's to stay on the bus till she gets to Eighth Street and Mr. Garland is going to meet her there."

By this time my entire body was wet with nervous perspiration. "But, Lelah," I broke in, "The Number Four Fifth Avenue bus doesn't go all the way down Fifth Avenue. It turns off at Thirty-third Street and ends up at Pennsylvania Station. Mr. Garland evidently thinks all Fifth Avenue busses end up at the same place."

Now Lelah was just as upset as I was. I asked her to think hard and tell me as nearly as she could how long it had been since Marcia had gone. Lelah said it must have been about ten minutes. I hung up the receiver and ran to Fifth Avenue, half a block away, where the familiar but now terrifying spectacle of endless lines of green Fifth Avenue double-decked busses confronted me. In one of these busses, somewhere still up Fifth Avenue, was Marcia, and somehow, some way I had to intercept that bus. Any father of a nine-year-old daughter can comprehend my feelings knowing what can happen to a little girl who might become lost among strangers in a big city.

Fifth Avenue is congested enough on an ordinary business day but this afternoon, just before Christmas, it presented a scene of indescribable confusion and activity. Hundreds of busses were en route downtown preparatory to taking out the home-going traffic as soon as the stores and offices should close at five o'clock. The day was dark with low overhanging clouds, a foggy mist in the air. In another half hour it would be dusk.

I was near panic as I jumped on the first Number Four bus to pass and asked the conductor what his ordinary running time was between 110th Street and Riverside Drive, where we lived, and this point on Fifth Avenue. He estimated it would take around thirty to thirty-five minutes but on a day like this, with traffic moving so slowly, it might take forty. I figured, at this rate, I might have a time leeway of possibly fifteen to twenty minutes before the bus carrying Marcia would reach Forty-fourth and Fifth Avenue. I had been carried all the way down to Thirty-third Street while talking to the conductor and I now jumped off the bus and ran back up the Avenue. If I was to locate Marcia, I would have to board the bus before it reached its transfer point at Thirty-third Street. There was an outside chance that Marcia might have told the conductor where she was going and that he had explained to her she would have to transfer to a Number Five at Thirty-third Street, but I could not count on this and I would have no way of knowing where Marcia would end up if I missed her.

The next ten minutes were the most harrowing I had ever experienced. I didn't dare let one Number Four bus pass me if I could help it without leaping on and looking for Marcia. I jumped one bus after another and would run down the aisle, glancing frantically from right to left, then I would climb the stairs to the upper deck and go halfway back to make sure that some large person had not blocked my little girl from sight. Each time I would be carried down the Avenue from two to five blocks and would fight my way off the crowded busses, crying: "Sorry—wrong bus! . . . Sorry—wrong bus!" leaving conductors and drivers and passengers shouting angrily after me.

Even with all my effort, I would get penned up in one Number Four bus and would see another of the same number pulling out and around me. Upset as I was, I could realize that this system wasn't going to work. It was taking too much time on each bus to make sure Marcia wasn't on it. If I could just know exactly where she was seated in the bus she was on, I would only have to board the bus, take one quick look at this spot and, if she wasn't there, jump off. But how could I ever determine this?

I stood on the corner of Thirty-sixth Street and leaned up against a lamppost, physically and nervously exhausted, a tight feeling in my head. If there was ever a time for my extra sensory powers to serve me, it was now. I tried to relax but, at first, my emotions would not let me. A fervent prayer took form in my mind. "God help me find Marcia!" Then the realization came over me that I MUST put all fears and feelings concerning Marcia out of my consciousness if I were to receive the impression where she was seated. I closed my eyes and became unmindful of the traffic and the crowds around me. In that inner stillness, I called, "Marcia—where are you? Where are you sitting?" And the answer came in a quick, clear mental picture. I saw her, in my mind's eye, seated happily and unconcernedly in the seat just above the stairs, all by herself.

As soon as this impression hit me, I knew it was right. Now, my only problem, still a big one, was to board the bus she was on. I looked at my watch. Time was running out. I mustn't miss any Number Four bus if I could help it.

In the next five minutes, I was on and off three busses, taking one look up the stairs. Marcia wasn't there and I turned immediately, forcing my way off. But I was trapped in the next bus I entered. As I saw that Marcia wasn't on it, another Number Four passed and I had a strong pulling sensation which told me unmistakably that this was the bus I must intercept. I pushed passengers aside, got to the closed door and banged on it, demanding to be let off. The driver said, "You'll have to wait until the next stop."

We were just approaching Thirty-sixth Street and the Number Four bus I needed to catch was already across it. I hit the door so hard with my knuckles that it cracked the glass and the driver, slowing down, half opened the door, yelling: "What in hell's the matter with you, Mister?"

I squeezed out, jumped to the pavement, ran ahead of the bus and down the middle of Fifth Avenue, dodging in, out and around slow moving traffic, with drivers shouting at me and horns honking. I paid no heed, my eyes centered upon the Number Four bus half a block ahead. It seemed, for a moment, as though I couldn't make it, and then the lights changed, stopping the bus at Thirty-fifth Street. I caught up to it and rapped on the door. The driver motioned irritatedly and said, "Next stop!"

"Open up!" I demanded. "Let me in!"

I banged on the glass so hard that he must have thought I would break it. He opened the door and started to bawl me out but I got in, shoved my way past several glowering passengers in the aisle, and looked up the stairs.

There, just as I had seen her in my mental picture, was *Marcia*.

When the conductor came for my fare, I asked for transfers, we boarded a Number Five bus at Thirty-third Street and rode to the end of Fifth Avenue, where Bob and Telly were to be waiting for Marcia. But the excitement and demands of the party had been too much for Bob—he wasn't there! You can be sure I was doubly glad and profoundly thankful that I had been enabled to find my little girl.

You can train yourself to recognize and follow what you call your "hunches" or intuition. This is the method that your inner mind uses to make you aware of things happening or about to happen beyond the reach of the five physical senses. By practice, you can learn to tell the difference between an intuitive and an imaginative or apprehensive feeling. When you have learned this difference, follow the direction of your intuition, even though it may seem foolish to your conscious mind at the time.

If you should sense something coming toward you in time as a result of your wrong thinking or a wrong combination of circumstances, you can avert it by a changed mental attitude and by taking the right course of action.

Your inner mind knows of ways and means and contacts of which your conscious mind has no knowledge. This is the reason that you should follow the intuitive urges you get out of a clear sky to do something, or go somewhere, or get in touch with someone. You can be sure, if you properly interpret your inner feelings, that you will always be led to better conditions and developments because they have been prepared for you by the God Power within, in answer to your own prayerful desires.

FIVE

The Reality of Thought

WHILE LIVING in Chicago, an experience came to me which demonstrated more than ever before the power of thought to create form.

A feature article had been published in the Chicago Daily News concerning my views on telepathy and life after death which brought me some hundreds of letters, among which was one from Mrs. Louise Fredendall, who expressed a desire to consult me on some unsought psychic experiences she had been having. I saw this woman and was impressed with her sincerity and intelligence as well as her possession of genuine sensitivity. I advised her to use caution in the development of these powers to avoid possible physical and emotional disturbance. Some months later, the Fredendalls moved to New York state and I received infrequent letters from her, reporting on different impressions upon which she desired my evaluation.

One day, as I was in the midst of dictating scenes of a play to Mrs. Sherman, my mind filled with the characters and situations, a letter came from Mrs. Fredendall which contained a warning that amused us greatly. She said she had had the strong feeling that some married woman of wealth and affluence had personal designs upon me. The further we read, the more certain we were that Mrs. Fredendall was entirely off the beam this time and had permitted her imagination to run wild. This was our opinion until the very last when she mentioned what she thought was this woman's name, and then we knew she had scored an amazing "direct hit." Herewith follows the exact words of her warning:

". . . A couple of mornings ago, I received an impression of a woman with whom you have been doing some work, and a warning about her.

She seems to be rather a large woman, of light complexion, quite full bosomed, well dressed and comfortably fixed financially. This woman, if not recognized by this description, may appear on your horizon in the near future. At any rate, I seem to see her presenting you with data, from time to time, with which you have been impressed. She is located where you can see her and vice versa. Her statements are apparently authentic and well stated and have interested you to the point of giving her your friendship.

Be careful! She is clever and uses your interest and friendly contact because she obtains certain physical stimulation from your presence. She had hoped to make greater inroads on your friendship, on a personal rather than business basis. Somewhat baffled by your reserve, she is proceeding slowly.

However, she has definite plans for a physical alliance.

I believe you to be totally unaware of this—in fact you regard her as a very nice person and one offering genuine evidence along the lines you seek. She did have a little to offer in the beginning and does very occasionally now. However, ninety-eight per cent of her "cases" are not authentic and she is being rendered "sterile" as far as such work goes and her reception is concerned, because her feet are in the clay. The discussion of her experiences has brought you together.

Cut her loose! Quickly! Later events will prove this to be right. Observe the desperate attempts of this person to see you on any pretext, if you do not see or talk to her, on the telephone, for a month. She will show her hand by her actions.

This woman is not the "loose" type. She has been married. She will cause you trouble and upset because she will be finally stung to desperation by your change in attitude, your lack of interest. Better that, which you will be able to bridge nicely, than what lies ahead.

Watch the rocks and bring your ship to port quickly and consider yourself lucky.

Is there possibly a LAURA involved in this in any way?

As I say, this may not be anything you can place now, but if not, please keep your eyes open.

However, I seem to feel that you already are quite involved with her and should you have already had misgivings and regrets, it positively is not your fault . . . You are inclined to be too kind and, being of an unusually sensitive and understanding nature, your love for humanity in general is many times misconstrued. You are most fortunate to have a wife who understands what you are really up against . . ."

I wrote Mrs. Fredendall, immediately, the following letter:

"Congratulations! You have made a remarkable direct hit! The woman's name is LAURA CAVENDISH—she is exactly as you have described her. This has been her attitude, she *does* have physical designs, and is interested in the occult, believing that she has psychic experiences—ONLY—Laura Cavendish is COMPLETELY FICTITIOUS!

For the past ten days I have been intensely concentrating on the writing of a new play, entitled "Hocus Pocus" (later given a stage production in Hollywood). I have been dictating this play to Mrs. Sherman and LAURA Cavendish has been almost constantly in mind. Some day, when I see you, I'll have to let you read a copy of the finished play to show you what an accurate mental pick-up you made. What you have done opens up a new avenue in thought transference which confirms what I have long contended: that thoughts are *things*—and a thought creation exists as realistically in mind as the thought picture of a real person.

The plot of my play concerns a Professor of Psychology and Philosophy in State College, whose wife joins a Seekers After Truth Society—a band of women who have gone overboard for

ISMS, such as Numerology, Astrology, Phrenology, Spiritism, Reincarnation and so on. In an attempt to demonstrate to these women how gullible they are, Professor Smith stages a fake trance, brings through an entity identified as "their Guiding Spirit," and gets himself proclaimed as a "Master" by the excited females who "Vibrate" his name and cast his horoscope and feel his head for bumps. The Professor then turns to his wife as a witness to prove to these women that he has tricked them, as he had told his wife he was going to do. But, to his consternation, LAURA Cavendish, the ringleader, wife of a wealthy banker, (the gushy, full-bosomed type as you indicated) declares: "Don't you believe him, Seekers. A great soul dwells within! Of course, now that the Professor has returned to his *mortal* self, he would deny his identity —but we have just had a wonderful demonstration of Professor Smith's psychic powers—and he is a Master, whether he realizes it or not!"

Thus, Professor Smith has unwittingly started a snowball rolling downhill which he cannot stop. The women drive him mad with their pestering him to see what psychic impression or guidance he can give them about every move they wish to make in life.

LAURA Cavendish develops a fixation on the Professor, annoys him by telephone calls and makes personal visits on every pretext (exactly as you felt) and—in a riotous scene, which I must have been dictating about the time you received your impressions, LAURA locks herself in the Professor's study with him, drops the KEY in the bosom of her dress so they won't be disturbed, and makes violent love to him—telling the Professor it was revealed to her in a dream that she had been Cleopatra and he, Mark Antony, in a previous incarnation—and that they were, in reality, SOULMATES.

When you picked up those impressions, you naturally visualized ME as the man in the case and felt that I should be warned against such a designing woman. When I read your letter to Mrs. Sherman, it did not dawn on us to whom you were referring —and you seemed far off—until you mentioned LAURA at the finish, which tied it all in."

The experience with Mrs. Fredendall recalls one of mine of a somewhat different nature, which occurred when I was first living in New York.

Edward F. Reimer was a tenant who resides on the same floor in our apartment house. We had become acquainted with the Reimers and occasionally spent an evening together.

One night I was over on Broadway, shortly after eleven o'clock, getting some writing supplies. As I was returning, within fifty feet of the 172nd Street corner, I saw Mr. Reimer emerge from 172nd Street and hurry to the mail box on the uptown corner of Broadway. He posted what I felt to be a special delivery letter, then turned about and hastened back. A drug store on the corner of 172nd Street and Broadway blocked my view of him.

Our apartment house was located at 735 West 172nd Street, two blocks over toward the Hudson River. Desirous of having Mr. Reimer's company home, I ran and turned the corner onto 172nd Street, expecting to catch up with him.

To my amazement, Mr. Reimer was nowhere to be seen! There wasn't a human on that side of the street in the entire block.

Somewhat bewildered, I tried to reason it out. After eleven at night there was no further mail pick-up at our corner of Haven Avenue and 172nd Street. But there were letter pick-ups from the Broadway boxes at midnight. Mr. Reimer evidently had an important letter to mail and that was why he had taken it over to Broadway. But WHERE had Mr. Reimer disappeared?

If I had mistaken someone else for Mr. Reimer, I would at least have seen that person on the street ahead of me. But there was no one, and not an apartment house door into which anyone could have gone.

Pondering this mystery, I continued on home and turned in at our apartment house. To my surprise, I encountered Mr. Reimer coming down the steps, letter in hand!

"Why, Mr. Reimer!" I exclaimed. "I thought I saw you just a few moments ago, mailing a special delivery letter at the Broadway corner!"

"No, it must have been someone else," said Mr. Reimer. 'But that's just where I'm going now, and this is a special delivery letter!"

He held it up for me to see.

"I can't understand it," I said. "I'd have sworn I saw you mail this letter on Broadway. I was only a short distance from you. But when I ran to join you, you had vanished from sight!"

"That's strange," he remarked. "I've been thinking of going to Broadway and posting this letter for the past ten minutes!"

"So you had it in your mind at the time I was actually on Broadway?" I asked.

"Yes," confirmed Mr. Reimer. "This is an important letter concerning a real, estate deal which must be received by tomorrow morning. That's why I'm sending it special."

I had no further comment to make but stood watching him hurrying toward Broadway, letter in hand. He did not look any more real to me now than he had appeared some five minutes before, when I hadn't actually seen him at all!

But what *had* I seen which so definitely resembled Mr. Reimer?

Had I intercepted his "thought intention" to mail that special delivery letter on Broadway? Had Mr. Reimer, without realizing it, projected a "thought form" of himself to that mail box which I had "tuned in on" and seen?

These experiences in extra sensory perception raise a profoundly interesting question: just what is reality? Where does the "real" end and the "unreal" begin?

Mrs. Fredendall could not distinguish in her mind between her reception of thought forms created in my consciousness of a woman who didn't exist and the images she had formerly seen of real life characters. I couldn't distinguish between the thought form of Mr. Reimer which I had perceived, and his actual physical form.

This leads to the wonderment—do children actually see people and things in their play which seem so real to them? Does their unrepressed imagination project thought forms which they, themselves, create for their own enjoyment, and companionship? They certainly see something, at times, just as I saw something, or, are forms from another dimension and plane of existence sometimes contacted by the extra sensory faculties of children, as well as adults?

This would seem to indicate that mind can create thought forms which have every resemblance to the pictures we carry in mind of real, live people. Authors often testify that the fictional characters they have created become so real and so powerful that they take over and dictate their own thoughts and acts, many times contrary to the original designs the authors have had for them.

This may tend to explain some of the self-created obsessions that men and women have experienced. Having committed a crime or an unpardonable sin, due to uncontrolled emotional and sexual drives, such individuals, in an attempt to salve their consciences and to escape moral responsibility, have created secondary characters and personalities within themselves, upon whom they place the blame.

They say, "John or Jane told me to do it," and hysterically or sullenly deny any direct connection with the misdeed. If they have not been apprehended by the law and this emotional and sexual drive has built up in them again, they repeat the crime, letting John or Jane "take over for the time being which frees them from all restraints of conscience or established morals. This is a tremendous field for Science to explore which can only be touched upon here.

I have studied mental cases and given much thought to the cause of confusion in consciousness. Since mental and emotional disturbances continue to be on the rise throughout the world, this is a subject which should be given paramount attention. For this reason, I would like to present a theory for consideration of all authorities associated with mental institutions as well as those readers of this volume who may have members of your own family or friends suffering from some mental or emotional disorder.

It is an acknowledged fact that the mind can think of only *one* thought at a time. I have stated that we think basically in pictures and not in words. When we speak, we express these words in sounds which are still only the symbols of what we see and feel in mind. In my opinion, the mental case whose words run together, who talks gibberish, and who has only occasional lucid moments, is an individual who has suffered what might be called a "short circuit" in consciousness. He has had an overwhelming emotional experience which has so shocked him that the motion picture machine of his mind has stopped at that point and is continuing to project a picture of this disturbed scene, upon which is superimposed whatever external situation this person may be facing at the moment. He is thus out of synchronization with his inner and outer self, his attention divided between a past and a present event, both of which are so distorted in consciousness that he has lost the power to discriminate between the real and the unreal.

When he tries to express in words how he feels in the present, he is so emotionally tied to this overshadowing past experience that his "sound track" runs together, which is what would happen if two films were laid, one over the other, and run through a projection machine, or two sound tracks dubbed upon the same recording. The only way such an individual can be freed from this unfortunate fixation is through capturing his conscious mind's attention by showing him scenes and pictures and providing experiences which have formerly had deep meaning and sentimental value for him. His constructive life experiences, love of home and friends and things, if this was in his background, must be presented in such a way that these feelings, reawakened, commence to take precedence over the one shattering experience which has stopped the normal functioning of consciousness. This method of treatment suggests the creation of an entirely new approach technique in dealing with many mental cases.

Other disturbed men and women are what might be termed "borderline sensitives," who have not learned how to insulate their minds against the strong thoughts of others, and have lost their sense of balance or control through association with dominating, critical, unloving, designing or immoral types of relatives and friends. Their supersensitivity has caused them to crack under such treatment where stronger personalities would have set up their own resistance and been little affected.

The possibility should also be explored that, in some instances, men and women may be truly obsessed by discarnate entities who have taken temporary residence in their consciousness, the door having been opened for their entrance through nervous breakdown or the excessive use of narcotics, alcoholics and the like.

It is a basic law of mind, still little understood, that what is created in consciousness always seeks externalization in some form. This is why some men and women who have led straight-laced lives, suddenly shock their communities by overt acts, seemingly entirely foreign to their natures. Their secret desires to commit such acts have been building up in them for years, intensified through repression, until finally these urges burst all bonds.

Of course, there are directly opposite cases wherein men and women, restricted by circumstances, finally respond to a long pent-up urge and break completely away from what they have been doing, startling friends and relatives by launching upon new careers and revealing abilities and powers of expression none had imagined them to possess.

What is in man must sooner or later come out or man shrivels up and dies on the vine of his own repressed desires. Whatever you want most to do, good or bad, you will ultimately do, if at all within your power. What you picture in your mind becomes a blueprint for the Creative Power within to work upon. There is great power in visualization.

SIX

The Power of Visualization

WHEN YOU plan something in advance that you hope to accomplish, you are actually creating that something in your mind. It will ultimately be just as perfected in consciousness as your past accumulated experience and acquired ability, applied to this objective, can make it. The Creative Power within can only help materialize for you in your outer world what you have built for yourself in your inner world. Basically, you must earn through your own physical, mental and spiritual effort whatever comes to you in life. This does not mean that your accomplishments will necessarily be well balanced or proportioned. You may possess what many term a "money sense" and operate the powers of visualization effectively in this field and yet operate very ineffectively on the plane of health, domestic relations and other vital phases of your life.

Each human has some blind spots in consciousness wherein his own mental and emotional reactions, like attracting like, are continuing to bring him wrong conditions and happenings. This can only be corrected by discovery of the cause and its removal, through elimination of the thoughts and feelings which have created it. The God Power within always helps, when called upon, but never dictates.

In seeking guidance of the God Consciousness, when you are visualizing what you desire to achieve, you must not try to force it. So many humans are so over-anxious to be led to do the right thing, to move in the right direction, to say the right thing, to see the right person, that they emotionally excite their imagination to produce ideas for them which, in their overzealous state, they mistakenly interpret as originating from the God Power within. Acting impulsively upon these self-created urges, they often come to grief and suffer a loss of faith in God and in themselves, afraid to follow what they thought had been their inner guidance from then on, feeling desperate, bewildered and alone.

Actually these distraught humans, with every good intention, had been trying to tell the God Power within what they, themselves most wanted to hear, glossing over, in many instances, their own weaknesses and inabilities which would have to be corrected by their own efforts before God could help them on the level of their desires. Had their attitude been less assertive and demanding, and had they asked that they might be shown what they needed to develop in their lives, what lack existed in them which had attracted a corresponding lack without, God would have spoken. The desire for self-illumination would have cut through the level of imagination and reached up to the level of God Consciousness.

It is difficult, when one is under economic and other emotional pressures, to assume and maintain an impersonal point of view, detached enough to see clearly your own possible mistakes and shortcomings which have been producing the very conditions from which you seek deliverance.

Faced with the problem which seems beyond you, and desiring help from the God Power within, you should concentrate during your meditation period upon composing your own mind and emotions, putting aside your fears and apprehensions and exercising the faith that when you have opened up the channels of your innermost being, the unmistakable answer to your prayers will flood your consciousness. Do not try to compel this answer to come at any specific time because the God Consciousness does not operate within the time limitations of earth. Your faith that you will know what is best to do at the time that is best for you, in relation to all other factors involved in your problem, will free the God Power to enter your life experience in a way that will be most helpful to you. Although you cannot sit down and wait for God to do things for you, it is wise to get off by yourself, take inventory, and see if you may not be doing things which are making it impossible for God to do anything for you.

The instant you see yourself, in your mind's eye, starting off on a new project involving other people and things, your thoughts make subconscious contact with all points visualized. It may take days or weeks before you make actual contact with these persons and things pictured, but they all exist in consciousness during your planning period just as realistically as though you had been in touch with them and, if your thinking with relation to them has been correct and constructive, you will, at the proper time, attract their association and cooperation to the end that what you have visualized and worked toward becomes an accomplished fact.

A few personal experiences will serve to illustrate:

In the middle 1930s, the idea came to me that I might dramatize, for radio, stage and screen, the life of America's great humorist, Mark Twain. Inquiry revealed that the rights to do this would have to be secured through the Mark Twain Estate, which had been established following Twain's death for the purpose of handling the sale and other business relative to his many literary properties. I found that this Estate was managed by an attorney, Charles T. Lark, with office on Fifth Avenue; that he was one of the trustees, and that he had been the lawyer who had drawn up Twain's will and acted as his executor. The Estate was being operated for Mark Twain's only surviving daughter, at that time, Mrs. Ossip Gabrilowitsch of Detroit.

I realized that my ambition to dramatize Mark Twain's life could not be achieved unless I was willing to invest my time and talent in preparation of a full and complete synopsis which might be presented to Mr. Lark in proof of my ability. It was evident that many writers of far greater reputation than mine had sought and were seeking the granting of these same valuable rights. I reasoned that these busy writers would perhaps not be willing nor have the time to prepare any material on speculation but would request these rights of the Estate based upon their established reputations. I therefore decided it was worth the gamble for me to devote all the spare time possible in a study of all writings on, about and by Mark Twain, to saturate my consciousness with his life activities and character, and then to prepare a detailed dramatic outline to show the Estate just how I would propose to handle this subject for the stage.

In preparing this work, which required about six months, I constantly pictured in my mind its acceptance by Mr. Lark and all concerned, when submitted. My conscious mind tried to suggest, at times, that I didn't have the ghost of a chance in competition with big name authors, that I was wasting my time, and that I was letting myself in for a major disappointment.

Intuitively, however, I felt that this project could succeed because I had a profound feeling of kinship for Mark Twain who, in his day, had recognizably used these same powers of Extra Sensory Perception. I hoped that Mr. Lark and Clara Clemens Gabrilowitsch and Albert Bigelow Paine, Twain's official biographer, who was then still living, would sense in the reading of my outline that my interest in Twain was not motivated by opportunism but by a deep conviction that my background and understanding could bring Twain to life in dramatic form.

When the outline was finally finished, I had it professionally typed and bound and, with that, I was now ready to make contact with Charles T. Lark for the first time. I phoned his office and made an appointment through his secretary. The night before keeping this appointment, in my period of meditation, I had what you might call an imaginary interview with Mr. Lark. I saw myself meeting and informing him of the purpose of my visit. I heard Mr. Lark explain politely to me that the Estate placed a high value upon the dramatic rights to Mark Twain's life and had turned down many offers and requests from authors. This information was not intuitive, it had been public knowledge. But, as I visualized my interview with Mr. Lark, I felt that the least he could say or do in appreciation of the time and labor I had put upon the script, would be to say that he would read it. If I could get him to agree to this much, in my first contact, I felt that this would be all that I could possibly expect.

During this meditation, a definite feeling came to me that Mr. Lark *would* agree to read the outline and, the instant I had this impression, I relaxed and went to sleep in the faith that all would go well with my appointment.

Everything *did* turn out exactly as visualized. Mr. Lark was much impressed by the enormous amount of work I had done on speculation, realizing, as I pointed out to him that, if he did not find my work acceptable, all he had to do was to drop the manuscript in the waste basket since I did not possess the rights and could go no further without legal sanction of the Estate.

The copyright laws are such that, while much of an author's writing and life may be in the public domain after his death, and following the expiration of his copyrights, as long as any living relatives remain who require dramatization as a part of any story, permission must be obtained from them or their Estate, for inclusion. In this case, Clara Clemens Gabrilowitsch as one of Twain's daughters, was to appear in several scenes.

Mr. Lark said frankly that he could give me no assurance whatsoever that all this work I had done would find favor with the Estate. He showed me a file of letters and telegrams from famous authors and producers, seeking these same rights. He said that Mrs. Gabrilowitsch wanted to make sure that her father's life would be tastefully and sympathetically dramatized and she did not wish to enter into any contract for such dramatization until she knew exactly how the playwright proposed to treat this subject. I left Mr. Lark's office with a light heart and a growing conviction that acceptance of my outline would be only a matter of time.

The waiting periods on any project are the hardest to endure. When you have done all you can, and the results are, as they say, "in the laps of the gods," having no word on how things are going, your conscious mind often upsets you by its fears and doubts and apprehensions. Since your conscious mind, in itself, has only the five physical senses to depend upon, it will try to impress you with the mathematical chances against success and all the human factors which might go wrong or rise up in opposition to a venture. I had my bad moments but found assurance in the meditation periods when, with the conscious mind's influence blocked out, my extra sensory feelings told me that what I desired would come to pass.

In about ten days, Mr. Lark's secretary phoned and asked me to mail to the office a copy of my bibliography. I knew from this that my outline was receiving serious consideration. Two weeks later, Mr. Lark, himself, called and invited me to lunch. He then reported that he had read the outline and had liked it so much he had mailed it on to the other trustees and Albert Bigelow Paine, and when he had received favorable replies from them, had sent the script to Mrs. Gabrilowitsch. She, too, had written, expressing her liking for the over-all treatment. "And I suppose now," concluded Mr. Lark, "what you want is the *go-ahead?*"

I told him it certainly was, that I desired to work in close association with the Estate in the dramatization and, after some discussion, the contract was agreed upon, granting me the exclusive rights in all dramatic forms.

Further evidence that much can be accomplished in and through consciousness which leads eventually to its materialization in actual life, is demonstrated in this experience:

I had been writing regularly for Boy's Life, the Official Boy Scout publication, for a number of years. Finally I arrived at the point where I felt I had earned higher remuneration for my stories, although the magazine was then paying me the top price allowed by its budget. I knew that my request for a raise would require a strategic approach in my friendly relations with Franklin K. Mathiews, editor. I therefore decided to discuss my case mentally with him as though he were actually present. I felt this would help me in talking personally to him later, so I sat down in my study and pictured myself in the presence of Mr. Mathiews, submitting my reasons for believing I was worth more to the publication than it was paying me.

I told Mr. Mathiews just exactly how much more I thought I should receive for each story. I seemed to hear him raising certain objections and explaining why the publication could not go higher. After further discussion, however, he seemed to concede that I was worth the amount I had proposed and said he would go before the budget board and see if he could make a special arrangement in my case. The moment I sensed that Mr. Mathiews had reached this decision,

I thanked him for his consideration and then dismissed the mental interview from consciousness, so that I would not reflect upon it with my conscious mind and give it a chance to undo, with its doubts and fears, what had now been accomplished by my subconscious.

It had been my intention to make an appointment with Mr. Mathiews to talk over this matter in the next few days, but each time I thought about it, I couldn't get the urge to take the initiative. While I was waiting for the right impulse, Mr. Mathiew's secretary phoned me. She said the editor was soon going to Florida and wanted to see me. Would I call at his hotel that afternoon? I did so, and was greeted by Mr. Mathiews with the statement that he had recently been reviewing the work I had done for Boy's Life, that he felt I was worth more money to them, and he had arranged with the Board for me to get it. Then, in asking if a certain raise would be acceptable to me, he named the very amount I had proposed in my mental interview.

It is occasionally possible to visualize for other people and to transmit thoughts which may reinforce or help change and strengthen their own mental and emotional attitudes. This is most effectively done during sleep. Children who have developed bad habits can often be reached in this manner. Sitting quietly by the bedside, after they have dropped to sleep, you can speak in a low voice, suggesting right conduct to them in a way to appeal to their sense of logic and liking, which thoughts will be received and put into operation by their subconscious.

Mrs. Sherman aided one of our daughters in overcoming the habit of thumb-sucking by this method when every conscious attempt, such as reprimands, painting the thumb with bitter solutions and even bandaging it, had failed. This daughter was told, during sleep, that she was changing the shape of her mouth by her thumb-sucking and she didn't want to do that because it was making her mouth unattractive. Response the next day was immediate and positive, as has been the response in many similar cases of self-help through suggestion.

Men and women who have a deep bond of sympathy and understanding between each other, can be of mutual assistance in visualizing the successful attainment of their respective desires. It is vitalizing for any person to know that some trusted friend or loved one shares this faith in himself and the God Power within. There is no limit to the power of visualization if supported by proper faith and the willingness to earn, through your own efforts, what you desire to achieve.

Perhaps the severest test of faith I have yet had in life came to me in the year 1935. I had been called in by the radio director of a large advertising agency to revise the format of a then famous musical show on the air. It was explained to me that, within the next several months, a streamlining of the entire program was to be made, and he wished me to prepare an outline for the new show and write the scripts. He stated that he could not give me a contract until the time should arrive for the change-over, and the present writers and actors, who were to be released, were freed of *their* contracts.

I foolishly accepted his proposal and went to work without even a letter agreement. Anticipating a lucrative engagement, I turned down other promising offers during this period but, when time came for my contract to be made, higher powers in the agency moved in, my ideas were given to other writers, and I sat at home, listening to my material, presented in revised form, go on the air. A theatrical attorney told me that I could sue and probably collect at least thirteen weeks' compensation, but he also advised that this case could be delayed in the courts and cause me more grief than it was worth despite the losses I had sustained as a result of this duplicity.

Several other ventures upon which I had put a great amount of work, also failed to materialize during this period, which culminated in our being compelled to leave our apartment. Although I had a good understanding of the operation of mind and emotions at the time, I found it impossible to prevent a venomous resentment rising up within me against this radio director who had preyed upon my time and talents so ruthlessly and caused me, as a consequence, such punishing economic embarrassment. This is the closest I have ever come to having murder in my heart for any human. But I paid dearly for my emotional disturbance.

One morning I awakened with a strange, smarting sensation spread over the membranes of my throat. Upon examination, I saw a white, cauliflower-like growth extending from the back of my tongue, over the sides of my throat and down over the tonsil areas. I could tell, at once, that this was some unusual affliction, and went immediately to my doctor who, never having seen this throat condition before, nevertheless diagnosed it correctly, as a mycosis. He gave me the grim information that there was no known specific cure and advised that I take the train at once to Philadelphia to consult one of the world's greatest throat specialists. My doctor stated that the history of such cases revealed this parasitical fungus growth to be most virulent, that within a few months' time, it could close the throat or extend into the ears, causing mastoids, or go down into the lungs—any one of these developments, of course, causing death.

At Philadelphia, cultures were taken for testing in the laboratory but nothing was done for ten days, except as I was rolled back and forth to the operating room for examination by different new doctors who studied these fungus growths through the bronchoscope and remarked, "How interesting!" (I later learned that outstanding throat specialists had been notified of this rare fungus growth and had flown in from other parts of the country just to have a look at it.)

At the end of these ten days, I was called into the famous specialist's office and informed that I could now return home to the care of my family physician. This was a bit difficult for me to understand since the fungus growth was still there, in fact had become extended to within a quarter inch of the windpipe. But I was informed that my family physician had been given instructions for my treatment.

Arriving back in New York, I went directly to my doctor's office. He was surprised to see me and asked my condition and what had been done for me. I told him that insofar as I could see, no treatment had been administered. And then I asked, "Haven't you heard from this specialist? He said he had written you."

My doctor shook his head. "No," he said, "I've had no word as yet. Let's have a look at your throat."

At about this moment, the postman came in with the morning mail which contained the promised letter. My doctor read it soberly and then passed it on to me. The specialist began by congratulating the physician for having correctly diagnosed the unusual mycosis. He then went on to state that they had been experimenting with cultures but had found nothing that had proved effective against them. The remainder of the letter, reading between the lines, was a polite return of the patient to die in the care of his family physician. When I had finished reading the letter, I turned to my doctor and said: "Well, where do we go from here?"

He said: "Harold, I've been making a study of these mycosis conditions while you've been gone and I know, as a chemist, that arsenic will kill both animal and vegetable life. Since this fungus growth is comprised of both, which accounts for its unusual virulence, most treatments that might work against one will usually not work against the other. So, with your permission, I propose to attack this parasitical fungus growth through your blood stream by injections of arsenic. By this method, I hope to check its spread and, eventually, kill it off. However, this is frankly experimental. It hasn't been tried on a human with respect to this mycosis, and it may not work."

I considered a moment but something told me to go ahead. I said, "It sounds good to me. I apparently don't have much choice. We've got to try something "

From then on, the battle began. Three times a week, I was the doctor's first patient in the morning and his last patient in the afternoon. He filled my blood stream as full of arsenic as he dared, and the fungus growth didn't like it. It commenced to retreat under the poisonous onslaught. It had been caked on my tongue almost half an inch high, in spots, and quite solidly down the sides of my throat, dangerously close to the windpipe, but, in a few months' time, under the arsenic attack, this growth was reduced to two spots, each about the size of a dime, directly over the area where my tonsils had been prior to an operation years before.

By this time I had taken so much arsenic into my system that the doctor was afraid its continued injections would injure other organs of the body. He said to me one day: "I think we'll do without these injections for a few weeks. Perhaps your body has now developed enough resistance to clear up this mycosis without any more arsenic."

We tried it and within a short time, the fungus growth began spreading like a prairie fire. I realized, then, that I was facing perhaps the greatest crisis of all. It had been proved that arsenic could check and control the growth of this fungus if it couldn't completely eliminate it. This meant that I appeared doomed to resume my arsenic injections in order to keep the mycosis from ultimately winning out. It meant also, that I must continue to endure the arsenic headaches which were so severe that I could hardly see and made any mental work next to impossible. However, I had no choice. I had to return to arsenic to save my life.

For just a moment, now, permit me to go back in time and give you an account of my emotional reaction to the realization that I had contracted this rare and unusual malady.

The first few days I was assailed by fear and apprehension. I had examined medical books and the unhappy pictures of men and women who had been afflicted with this same fungus growth which, in a few months' time, uncontrolled, had closed off their windpipes, bringing about suffocation. No operations were possible because the presence of this mycosis in the blood stream would mean death. The medical records showed that some forty known cases in the past fifty years had all succumbed. It was understandably difficult for me to lift my mind above such a realistic percentage against me. I had a wife and two daughters and other family responsibilities, and was in no economic condition to leave them with any security.

But, aside from all this, which bore heavily upon me, I had a tremendous desire and will to live. For the first few nights when I entered upon my meditation periods, I found it impossible to concentrate or control my feelings. Fear took over and caused me to see nightmarish pictures of myself awakening in some future moment, coughing and choking, with the realization that the growth had reached my windpipe and that my life was soon to be cut short.

Coupled with these fears, I discovered, was an intense and burning hatred of the radio director who had started my cycle of misfortune. Then, suddenly, as I fought to gain control of my emotions, it came over me with devastating conviction that my hate for this man had so filled my system with poison that it had changed the chemistry of my body and made it susceptible to the contraction of this fungus growth, which otherwise would probably have never been attracted to me.

I recalled my doctor having asked on my first visit if I had recently eaten any moldy bread. It so happened that Mrs. Sherman had discovered mold on a loaf of bread we had partially eaten several days before, and had thrown the remainder away. The doctor explained that many humans are taking molds of one kind or another into their bodies every day but this usually has no effect upon the organism. In my case, for some strange reason, the fungus had taken hold.

After this reflection, I was convinced that I knew the reason—that I had set up the cause of my affliction within myself, and that I would have to aid medical science as much as I humanly could by striving to eliminate from my mind and my body the destructive effects of my own thinking and feeling. I would have to stop picturing my condition as hopeless and, each meditation period, I would need to work on myself in an effort to remove the deep-seated feelings of bitterness toward this radio director.

Gradually, as I regained my mental perspective, I could see that I basically had my own self to blame and not the man for the advantage he had taken of me. This did not excuse his weakness and dishonesty but if I had employed good business sense in demanding a letter of agreement so it would not have been my word against his, I would have had something in writing to show for my work, and he would have been compelled to treat me fairly.

This shifting of the blame for my unhappy experience helped me to develop, in time, a forgiving attitude toward him and even, incredibly, a degree of good will. But, in addition to this, as I considered my own serious physical condition, I felt that I must do something to combat the recurrence of fear which lurked in the background of consciousness at all times.

One evening, there came to me in a period of meditation, from some extra sensory source, a strong feeling that there was, somewhere in this world, an individual who knew a specific remedy for this form of mycosis. It was almost as though I had made subconscious contact with this person in my need. My problem, if this impression was true, was to find that individual—to be drawn to him or he to me. A great surge of hope rose up in my consciousness. I thought, "If I can free my mind of hate and fear and other destructive feelings, then I will be able to picture, instead, with faith and confidence, that I will meet someone, some time, somewhere, who will know a specific cure for this mycosis, in time to save my life."

Once I decided upon this visualization, it became almost an obsession with me. I lived in the constant expectation of meeting this individual. It was my last visualization at night and my first on awakening. I did not try to force it. I kept repeating, ". . . in time to save my life" and felt that the God Power within would synchronize my movements in time and eventually bring what I had pictured to pass. This persistent faith buoyed me up through all the setbacks and trying months that followed. And, even when I was confronted with the necessity of having more arsenic injections to keep this fungus growth confined to the tonsil area, I still felt, unexplainably, that release was going to come.

In all the time I had been combating this affliction I had kept the knowledge of it from even my closest friends. There was nothing external to indicate that I was in any trouble aside from the necessity for me to clear my throat quite often. It was my feeling that if the news should get around that I was suffering from this fungus growth which was supposed to be incurable, and if my friends accepted the concept that I might not be long for this world, I would have to fight their negative thinking along with my own. Consequently, only my wife, mother and doctor knew what I was undergoing.

One day, Sydney Este, a friend who shared my interest in metaphysical subjects, asked if Mrs. Sherman and I would like to attend a lecture to be given by a Dr. A. E. Strath-Gordon on "The Great Pyramid of Egypt." He told me that Dr. Strath-Gordon had been a brain surgeon for the British Government during the World War and that he had served on a Commission in the early 1900s which had entered and studied the Great Pyramid. We attended the lecture and found the talk of great interest but Dr. Strath-Gordon even more so. I felt strongly drawn to him for some reason and stayed to meet him afterward, inviting him, on impulse, to lunch with me at the City Club the following day.

When we met over the dining table, I was eager to discuss many subjects with him, but had a spell wherein I was compelled to clear my throat several times. Dr. Strath-Gordon observed me quietly and remarked: "You appear to be having a little trouble with your throat."

Heretofore, if someone had made such a comment, I had brushed it aside but now I felt the urge to confide the difficulty I had been having, to this new friend. He showed immediate interest and requested that I give him the history of my case and the condition of my throat at the present time. I told him that, thanks to the arsenic, this fungus growth had again been limited to two small areas where my tonsils had been but was so deeply rooted to the membranes at these points that it had resisted all attempts to dislodge it.

Dr. Strath-Gordon said, "Do you have pencil and paper?"

Wonderingly, I produced a pencil and the back of an envelope.

"Take down this prescription," he directed, and then commenced to dictate the ingredients, "so many parts of creosote . . . so many parts of glycerine . . . so many parts of this and that . . ."

When I had finished copying, I looked up at him and asked: "Just what is this prescription, Doctor?"

"It is a specific for your type of mycosis," he said, simply.

"But how—where did you get it?" I wanted to know, almost unbelievingly.

"Years ago," said Dr. Strath-Gordon, "I was sent by the British Government to work with Noguchi, the famous Japanese scientist, in South Africa. While I was there, this mycosis, which thrives in hot, humid climates, became epidemic, and the natives were dying like flies. Noguchi developed this solution and if it was applied before the fungus growth became too extensive, it saved their lives."

I was like a man emerging from a dream. Here, at last, seated across from me, was the person I had visualized meeting all these weeks, someone who knew a specific cure for my ailment. My extra sensory perception had been right. There had been an individual who carried the knowledge of a cure in his consciousness and I had finally been drawn to him out of all the human beings in this country.

"Doctor," I said, "do you mind if we cut short our visit at this time? I would like to take this prescription, at once, to my doctor, and try it out."

"By all means, Sherman," smiled Dr. Strath-Gordon, "we can meet again some other time."

I took a taxi to my doctor's office, related the remarkable circumstances which had placed this prescription in my hands, and asked him what we should do about it.

"Get the prescription filled at the nearest drugstore," he said.

When I returned, my doctor took an applicator, saturated it with the solution and swabbed my throat over the affected areas. There was a stinging sensation, the remaining growths shriveled up and dropped off—and I was cured.

You can increasingly understand, I am sure, why I believe so deeply in the power of visualization. If you will check back in your own life, you will discover that it has been of equal service to you, perhaps without your conscious realization, because everything that happens to you has to have had its origin in mind

You can learn to employ the power of visualization even more effectively if you will conscientiously follow the practices I have herein outlined. Every successful man and woman has been a positive visualizer.

What problem are you facing today? What unrealized aspiration do you have? Start picturing what you want and need. Repeat this visualization over and over, day after day, with faith in the God Power within, and faith in your own efforts. Persist and fulfillment must eventually come.

SEVEN

The Power
of Healing

SOMEONE HAS said, "Good health is largely a state of mind." Science today has proved this to be startlingly true. Your mind has far greater influence upon every cell of your body than was dreamed of, even a few years ago. The basic origin of many so-called diseases and afflictions, is now being traced to mind. Doctors say, "to heal the patient, we must treat his mind as well as his body."

A short time ago, an astonishing, frank confession was made by a study group representing the American Psychiatrists Association and the Association of Medical Colleges in New York. This group, after an exhaustive survey, made this statement:

"Doctors today know a lot about disease but too little about *people*—and what makes them chronically ill. Doctors are failing to satisfy the *emotional* needs of people by treating their clientele as mere patients, rather than as fellow human beings."

The report went on to say that, with the modes of life changing so rapidly in this country, many men and women are responding to strain by suffering a break in health. Doctors were therefore urged to *study people*—how they live—so they could determine the factors which were bringing about tension and unhappiness.

Now, as you know, I am not a doctor, but I have been studying people all my life. And because of this, I know how you live, how you think, how you feel—how you are apt to react to the different experiences you are having each day.

Why wait for the doctors to make a study of *you*? Start now and make a study of—*yourself*. Discover what's wrong with your thinking and your emotional reactions to life.

You can prevent the causes you are setting up in yourself, through wrong thinking and wrong emotional reactions, which will, one day, bring about ill health and unhappiness, unless corrected.

Remember, I have said that, in the mental world, "like attracts like"; that, as you picture in your mind and in your heart, so are you. The more deeply you feel, the more deeply you desire, the more deeply you fear—the more certain you can be that what you feel or desire or fear—is going to happen.

That is why I counsel you to watch your thinking and your emotions—because what you picture today, with real feeling behind it, can become a reality tomorrow.

The medical profession is fast giving recognition to this fact—to the tremendous part that your mind and emotions play in the state of your health and the conditions of your life.

Just recently, Dr. Lauren T. Guy, in a report made to the Medical Society of the County of New York, declared:

"Worry and tension can lead to blindness, and bring on glaucoma."

He then continued by recommending that "a realistic analysis by the *patient* of his personal problems could do more to relieve him of his physical disorders than fretful worrying, and be far less harmful to eyes, heart, blood pressure and other affected organs."

Accepting Dr. Guy's statement, it should then be obvious to you, if worry is the cause of physical ailments, the best preventative is to learn how to avoid worry.

Worry has been defined as "that state of mind which leads some persons to fear, every time the tide goes out, that it will never come in again," and the tide won't come in for you, as long as you picture it staying out. You will demagnetize the very conditions about you which you would ordinarily attract by a positive mental attitude.

A woman in New York was so crippled with arthritis that she couldn't walk. The only way she could get about was to crawl around on her hands and knees. They brought her in a wheelchair to a "self-development" class I was presenting. She heard me say that many illnesses were caused by wrong thinking, wrong emotions, that harboring bitterness or resentment changed the chemistry of the body, that it made a person susceptible to illnesses which would otherwise not be attracted (as in the case of my throat condition).

She told me that now she could see how she had brought this condition on herself; that her son had humiliated her, he had not turned out as she had hoped. She had feared, when a boy, that he would get in wrong company and commit crimes because he was so headstrong. Surely enough, as a young man, he *had* gotten into trouble. After that, she had tried to control his every thought and action. He had rebelled and gone from one crime to another.

She said: "Mr. Sherman, my husband and I had never had a breath of scandal connected with our names My son's conduct disgraced us and I couldn't forgive him for that. I felt terribly bitter toward him—I still do. How can I help it?"

It wasn't easy to tell this mother that she had, unwittingly, by her too condemning and dominating attitude, helped bring the very condition she had feared on her boy. And then, becoming so emotionally upset, she had brought this arthritic condition upon herself.

When realization came, even so tragically late, this woman went to work on herself. She released, in time, all bitterness from her mind, forgave her son as she hoped to be forgiven, and, in three months, the arthritic condition was gone. This woman is, today, helping others overcome their own wrong thinking.

Are you nursing any feelings of bitterness or resentment or hate or jealousy toward anyone? Does any person or thing or activity irritate you? If so, you may expect some irritation to show up in your body, because your body, sooner or later, reflects the irritations of your mind.

A man in my class in Seattle was going blind. He had only thirty percent vision. His blindness had baffled the doctors. They could find no physical cause. This man heard me say that blindness and deafness were often brought about in men and women who did not want to face something in life, who wanted to avoid seeing or hearing certain persons and things.

"Mr. Sherman," this man asked, "when I wake up each morning, I can see clearly for five or ten minutes, and then my vision gets clouded. Can you explain this?"

I said to him: "I think I can. You have just revealed to me by this statement that your trouble is mental and emotional—not physical. You're not really blind at all but, subconsciously, you want to be blind to the world of reality. When you awaken, you are able to see but the instant you realize that you have returned to consciousness, the thing or person you don't want to see or face comes to mind—and you lose your sight. You haven't confessed this to your doctors but you are greatly disturbed about something in your personal life. Isn't this so?"

"Yes," said the man, "I haven't wanted to admit it— but it is."

"Then I can say to you," I replied, "that you won't recover your sight until you have removed this emotional block from your mind. But the moment this is done, you will see again!"

It took the man a few days to decide to free his mind of the disturbance. Then he came to me and told me a poignant story of domination by his mother, a domination so complete and devastating that it had ruined his business and domestic life. He hadn't known how to break the emotional hold his mother had on him. He wanted to get away from her; he didn't want to see her again; he didn't know how to face the situation. So, his attempted escape, as he now began to understand, had taken the form of blindness.

Once the consciousness of this man was cleared, his eyesight cleared up. But, for a time, his vision would blur whenever he would get emotionally upset.

What are you worrying about? Is it something actually ridiculous when you analyze it? Right thinking, control of your emotions, the proper expression of faith and effort, can accomplish what the world still considers miracles.

My first outstanding experience with the healing power of mind took place in Detroit in August of 1920, when I was a young man employed by the Ford Motor Company.

Playing tennis, one day, I developed a water blister on the toe next to my big toe on the right foot. I didn't take it seriously but a few days later my toe became infected, highly inflamed, and badly swollen. Dr. Garner, my family physician, lanced the toe but it grew steadily worse. Within a few days, I had developed gangrene. The pain was excruciating. I lost twenty pounds in a short time and my fever mounted to 106 degrees. Dr. Garner became alarmed and called in a specialist, one evening, for consultation. It was decided that if my foot was no better by the next morning, it would have to be amputated. The specialist feared I might have to lose more than the foot.

Asking Dr. Garner to remain a few minutes after the specialist had left, I said to him: "Please tell me, frankly, what are my chances?"

His reply was: "Harold, as of now, they don't look too good, but I'm hoping you'll have a change for the better by morning. It wouldn't be wise to wait any longer than that."

In this critical moment, I felt impelled to make an unusual request of Dr. Garner. My studies of mind had convinced me that, if one could picture a healthy condition of body clearly enough and strongly enough, he could materially aid his recovery from many illnesses. I had secretly been trying, for the past few days, to picture my gangrenous toe restored to normal but, each attempt I had made to relax body and mind, and place this picture in consciousness, I was so aware of the pain and the present condition that all I could see and sense, in intensified form, was the infected toe, itself. What I needed, it now occurred to me, was the additional power of a healthy mind in a healthy body.

"Dr. Garner," I said, "I have the feeling that I can lick this thing but I can't do it alone. You may not understand this or agree with my conviction, but I'd appreciate it if, when you go home tonight, you would sit quietly for a few minutes and picture in your mind what has to happen to my toe to make it well." I then explained to Dr. Garner my own mental efforts to help improve my condition and added, "Please don't say you'll do this, if you don't mean it. Don't kid me or it won't do me any good."

Dr. Garner said to me, "If you think it will help, I'll be glad to do it. How much time would you like me to give to it?"

"Could you give me half an hour?" I requested.

"You *have* half an hour," he said. He told me he had one other call to make but expected to be home at ten o'clock and would concentrate on me, as directed, from ten to ten-thirty.

When he had gone, Mrs. Walker, my landlady, who had been standing concernedly in the doorway, said to me: "Harold, would you mind if I thought along with you tonight?"

"Mrs. Walker," I replied, "I would appreciate it very much. I am going to need all the help I can get."

She was a woman who believed in mental science, and her offer to think for and with me buoyed my spirits. I could hardly wait for ten o'clock to arrive and, when it did, I relaxed my body as best I could and made my mind passive. Then-, as I had tried countless times before, I sought to see a picture in consciousness of a healthy toe. Instead, all that registered was this toe in its infected state. The toe had been so swollen and so painful that I had not been able to bear a bandage upon it. Even the gentle lowering of a sheet upon my toe could not be endured.

I knew that Dr. Garner, in his home, and Mrs. Walker, nearby, were both visualizing, so I let go of this wrong picture and tried again and again but, each time, the picture was unchanged. It was twenty minutes past ten when, suddenly, it seemed as though I had tuned in on the positive thoughts that were being projected toward me. For just an instant, I glimpsed a fleeting picture of my toe as it had been before the infection. The mental relief was so great that I fell asleep and slept the night through for the first time since this gangrene had developed.

I awakened in the morning at six, my first thought one of apprehension lest I might bump my toe against something I lifted my foot carefully and was amazed to see that it had broken open during the night and drained and was now healed over. It was still somewhat discolored but the swelling was almost gone and I had no pain. Not only that, I had no fever.

I sat up on the edge of the bed and tested my foot against the floor, then carefully stood up and risked my weight upon it. There was no discomfiture. I went to the closet, stepped into my slippers, put on my bathrobe and broke the almost unbelievable news to Mrs. Walker. When Dr. Garner arrived at eight o'clock, prepared to take me to the hospital, I met him at the door.

It was several months before my toe was completely returned to normal but the crisis had passed that night and an undeniable healing had taken place through the creative power of mind. Later, when I told a few friends of this experience, two of them expressed doubt and asked permission to write Dr. Garner, relating the details as I have presented them here, and soliciting his comment. I have seen his letters in reply. He said, in effect: "It is true, what Harold Sherman has told you, about his recovery from gangrene. In my more than forty years of medical practice, this was the nearest thing to a miracle that I have seen."

We are still in the infancy of our knowledge concerning the healing possibilities of the Creative Power in mind, rightly directed. We know, beyond any doubt, that wrong feelings and emotional reactions can and do upset your health and that, as previously stated—fear, anger, hate, resentment, jealousy—and all of these kind of feelings can make you sick—can poison your mind and body.

If you are ill in body or mind at present, the chances are it is due to some past, unhappy emotional experience, a wrong mental attitude which is still in consciousness and which needs to be discovered and removed to bring about a correction of this condition. It will do you little good to picture yourself recovering from a condition unless you feel a deep inner assurance that what you are picturing will become a reality—is even now a reality in mind.

To solve your own health problems, you must be able to have absolute faith in the source from which you expect a healing, whatever that source of healing may be. It is my conviction that medical science has much to contribute to the health of mankind and that we should make intelligent use of all that is within and without ourselves which can add to our state of health at any time.

It is well to remember that God is working through the minds of all humans and can make contact, through mind, with the humans you need to meet who possess what you must have to aid or completely alleviate your condition. In any event, you must have a knowing faith that whatever you are picturing and doing is leading to the recovery of your health. But your basic source of healing will always be your God-given creative power within.

Consider, for a moment, how amazing this creative power is on the physical plane alone. From the instant you were conceived, this creative power took charge and ordered the rapidly multiplying millions of cells to make up the different organs of your body. Your creation was directed according to blueprint specifications in the building of the house you now occupy.

What is generally not realized is that this creative power is just as much a part of you today as it was when you were first conceived. It is constantly at work directing the creation of new cells to replace old ones which are dying, repairing body tissue which has been injured or worn out, healing different conditions as needed, and keeping your vital organs, every part of your body and brain functioning.

But this creative power, having provided you with your body, is now influenced by and takes its orders from your mind. The mental pictures you give it, dependent on their character, are materialized into good health or bad.

If when in poor health you could picture the recreation of your body, vividly and earnestly enough, with complete faith, I am confident an almost instant healing would result. In my opinion, this is the explanation of such remarkable healings as doctors testify have taken place at such shrines as Lourdes in France. The men and women who received healings of such conditions as cancer, tumorous growths and the like, saw themselves being healed in their mind's eye, with such ecstatic feeling of faith and yearning, that the God-given Creative Power within them was activated to so energize the cells in the physical areas affected, that re-creation occurred at once, and instantaneous healings were the result.

Few of us have developed the capacity for such exercise of faith. Most of us have to accomplish similar results, when we can, by a faithful repetition of the right mental pictures and a persistent exercise of faith, to the end that this creative power within is given sufficient impetus to perform the healing or attract the proper healing aid to us.

It is truly the God Power working in us when this happens, but we are the ones who, through right thinking, have to set it in motion. Especially is this true when it is our wrong thinking which has created wrong conditions in us.

Once we have been created, it is important to realize, we, as creatures of free choice and free will, have become, henceforth, our own creators. Fear and doubt can destroy in a short time what you may have taken weeks or months to build up, so don't permit feelings of despair and discouragement to take possession of you. If you do, they will impress this creative power within you to work against you instead of for you.

The key to your improved health is the confident inner expectation of recovery which you carry in your own consciousness.

EIGHT

The Power
of Your Personality

OUT OF the Great Within has come the Great Without and what you see in the Great Without today is but a reflection of the Great Within. This being true, the Great Within must change first before the Great Without can change. The most important work of the world is with the minds of men because the Great Within is in stupendous upheaval. Out of it is coming the pent-up hates and resentments of mankind which have been repressed for centuries.

The God Consciousness, at the core of the Great Within, is stirring the minds of men as they gain an awareness of it and aspire to higher material, physical, mental and spiritual attainments. But when great masses of humans are moving in directions seemingly opposed to yours, it is often difficult to see anything of God in them. Yet each human of every race and color must possess the same basic kinship, the same possibility of conscious attunement with the God Power within him that you, yourself, possess. He may not have reached your state of awareness. He may lack, for the time being, any evidence of the existence of the God Consciousness but it is there, nevertheless, awaiting his discovery.

To understand humanity, you must realize that everything re-volves around the Self. Every individual has a magnetic center at-tracting to himself, through the nature and quality of his visualiza-tion, what he feels he wants. The wants of the vast majority of humans will always decide, at any given time, the kind of world you live in and the forms of government which rule over this world. There is a self-interest in every person so strong that it will rebel, eventu-ally, against any force or institution that seems to be out of sympa-thy with it or opposed to its desires. No two humans want exactly the same thing at the same time. There is always a measure of con-flict even in the most harmonious relations. The germ of discon-tent is necessary to bring about a desire for progress and even finer associations.

The eternal urge for human advancement and expansion comes from the God-ward side of man. He knows, intuitively, that he has not begun to tap his capacities. He overcomes one obstacle and immedi-ately starts looking for a bigger one to surmount. The creative drive will not let him rest. It keeps saying to man, "Do something more with yourself. Don't be satisfied where you are. There are finer achievements ahead." And man responds, often blindly, to the compelling desire to meet the challenge of living and rise to higher levels of creature com-fort and satisfaction by so doing.

But man's tendency, thus far, has been to lose himself in the realm of his feelings. His destructive emotions have overwhelmed his reason and judgment at critical times and turned man against himself as well as his fellow humans. This is why the development of emotional con-trol and the elimination of violent hates, resentments and prejudices are so absolutely imperative if humans are ever to live peacefully with one another.

You can never force your concepts of your way of life upon any human, anywhere, unless he will open his mind and heart to them; un-less these concepts honestly appeal to his sentiment and his logic. Na-ture has set up an insulation about the mind of each individual which ordinarily protects that consciousness from the trespassing, intrud-ing or vagrant thoughts of others. This protective shield, surrounding consciousness, is not violated except as you become emotionally or mentally unbalanced and thus susceptible to the influence of strong thoughts and feelings from without.

What is consciousness?

It is a state of awareness—an awareness of BE-ING.

In the beginning, this state of awareness must have been entirely Subconscious. All things existed but no thing had an individual consciousness of existence. All was energy and motion without form or shape. The whole of infinitude was locked in one incomprehensibly gigantic thought. That thought was God and His expression of it brought about Creation.

Because the Original Thought is Timeless and Spaceless, it exists forever. Creation is, therefore, a never-ending, eternal evolvement of the God Consciousness in all things, high and low, seen and unseen, animate and inanimate, everywhere and anywhere present, on earth and throughout the infinite dimensions of God's ever-expanding universe.

God, in giving expression to Himself, brought form into being as a reflection of that Self. In this manner, God became manifest to Himself in and through what we now call Nature. Thus, thought and substance are one, and neither can exist without the other. Creation is the continuous, ever-changing union of thought and substance. And Life is God's entitized awareness of His existence in all parts of His Universal Being. But, because God is infinite in His expression, it follows that the forms of His expression must also be infinite. And, because these forms are constantly undergoing change as they react to environment and experience, it is evident that God, Himself, in His Outward Manifestation, is evolving with His own Creation. This is the only way in which God could grant Free Will expression, within the limits of the laws of His own Being, to all parts of His creation.

As a human part of this creation, you are then destined to participate with God in the development and evolution of your own soul and being as your contribution toward the perfection of the Universal Whole. You are, whether you yet realize it or not, a spark of the Divine, struck off on the anvil of creation, given life and identity in God, the Father-Mother of all things. And you and you alone must fan this spark, through the fire of your own experience, until that day when conscious awareness of the God Presence within you is attained.

From that moment on, you will leave the world of your lower senses behind and enter upon a plane of existence provided by God, the Great Intelligence, as the next step toward increasing self-at-one-ment with Him and the matchless wonders of eternal unfoldment to come.

Born out of the Great Subconscious, you are launched upon the sea of life in eternal quest of the ever greater Super Conscious. From the instant God gave expression to Himself, you came into existence as a Subconscious part of Him. The God force was not conscious of you as an entity but in the inconceivable concatenation of causes and effects which were set up in that instant, you were destined, one day, to make your appearance at some point in the universal scheme of life.

Where you were to appear, or when, or in what form, was to be determined by the infallible laws of attraction and repulsion, acting and reacting in such a manner that there would come a time when an infinitesimally small but infinitely promising part of God, the Great Intelligence, would encase itself in a physical instrument and become the point of awareness that is you.

Everything that has not become a conscious part of existence is still resident in the Great Subconscious. It remains to be unfolded and externalized in some future moment of what we call Time. Thus, what fails to take place today, through accident or obstruction, only awaits the favorable combination of circumstances to bring it ultimately into being. If you had not come into existence at the time you did, that portion of the God Consciousness which you represent and exclusively are, would have been called into existence upon some future occasion when the specific vibratory conditions demanded *your* externalization, and none other.

God has an eternity in which to express Himself, and there is no limit to the number and character of evolving individualized beings who may emerge from the Great Subconscious, in the timeless future, to join with you on the endless journey toward greater and greater understanding of self and the relation of that self to the God Presence within.

But all of these journeys begin with the entrance of each entity into form. As you study God's handwriting in Nature, it is revealed to you that the evolution of so-called lower forms of life developed for you, through untold aeons of time, the highly sensitized physical instrument which your entity now indwells.

Before you could manifest on your level of being, with the consciousness that is yours, it was necessary that Nature should develop and provide for you a body adapted to your needs. Until such a body was evolved, the consciousness indwelling its more primitive forms functioned on the instinctual animal level with no self-awareness and no recognition of identity.

Today, you are the inhabitant of a body form which came originally from the sea and which, long since, has divested itself of gills and, much later in its evolutionary life, as a land animal, left off its tail. You have been subconsciously attached to this unbroken chain of evolving descendants from the first moment of germ life on this planet until the time came for your physical appearance on this earth in the specific creative act of your parents. They had no power to provide you with life. This, you already possessed from the first moment of creation in common with all beings then created, only an infinitesimal portion of whom have yet become manifest or can ever become manifest in the boundless unfolding of God's Eternal Expression.

You became conscious of life with the leaving of your Subconscious existence and the taking on of your present body form. Prior to this time, it might be said that you had slept progressively in the consciousness of your real Father-Mother, God, awaiting the moment of your individual awakening in form to a self-conscious awareness of your being.

There is buried now in your own subconscious, itself still related to the Great Subconscious, a microcosmic record of your own evolution throughout the unthinkable ages that have passed up to the present moment. Instinctively and intuitively, you get fleeting feelings and fragmentary visions, awake and asleep, of past events in the long, long life span of this mysterious creature who calls himself, "Man."

You know, as yet, so very, very little about yourself —of who and what you are, of why you are here, and of where you are going. You are almost totally unacquainted with the nature of the *house* in which you live, and you know even less about its tenant—*yourself.*

It is only yesterday since the creature that is now Man, first stood erect amid the beasts of the jungle and asked the self-same questions: "Who am I? What am I doing here? Where am I going?"

When the consciousness of Man first emerged from the Great Within and entered the Great Without, Man was overwhelmed by what he saw and sensed about him. He found that he possessed in his body five physical senses—sight, hearing, taste, touch and smell—through which he was to interpret all things outside himself. The wonderment as to who he was and from whence he had come was overshadowed by the fight he had to make for survival in the wilderness of Nature and the wildness of all life about him. Yet Early Man intuitively knew, as he fought to conquer his environment and to elevate himself above all other forms of life on this planet, that he was not as other animals.

He knew this from the moment that his body form had become sufficiently refined and sensitized by evolutionary development to enable the consciousness of self to function through it. Everything had been subconscious up to then but, with the breaking through of conscious awareness, individual identity came into being and began its experience in human form. All physical forms of life are simply transmitting and receiving instruments for the species which indwell them, so designed by the Creative Power to serve each species in accordance with its need and capacity at any given moment. For the consciousness that is Man to manifest, a highly sensitized physical instrument was demanded of Nature. And even today, as Man's mind and soul evolve, his physical instrument must keep pace.

This means that new sensory faculties which Man has always possessed, in a largely undeveloped and usually unrecognized state, must come into being to augment the five physical senses which are no longer adequate to enable him to interpret the world outside and within himself of which he is now becoming increasingly conscious. All that Man ever is or can be is contained in his own subconscious. He possesses undreamed of powers which are only awaiting discovery and development by him.

This is your heritage. The sum total of all Man's experience from the dawn of identity in Man is contained in the vast subconscious of the human race. You bear a kinship in consciousness with every human creature who has ever lived as will all humans who follow you in this life. You are the sole possessor of your individual identity and personality, and no human creature, either before or after your existence here, has had or will have an identity or personality or even a physical appearance exactly like yours. You are unique in the universe, designed for a specific place and function which it is your free will choice to occupy and perform.

Today, as Man, you have emerged from the primitive jungles into a maze of civilized complexities. Looking back, you can view the panorama of Man's struggle to understand himself throughout the ages, his grievous inhumanities to his fellow man but, with it all, his search for something higher and finer in and beyond Man.

Out of the past, great spiritual leaders loom up whose thoughts and teachings have influenced millions down to the present day. The long night of superstition and ignorance is almost over. You are alive at a time when an unbounded opportunity exists for your attainment of true knowledge of self and the knowing attunement with the God Consciousness within. Science is confirming, in many instances, the truths of what Man has long professed by faith. That higher sensory faculties exist in the mind of Man, is no longer denied.

In the face of this steadily accumulating evidence, from earliest recorded time up to the present moment, that Man possesses undoubted higher powers of perception far beyond the reach of his comparatively crude five physical senses, the most incredible fact is the lamentable tardiness of Science in its investigation, recognition and evaluation of these powers.

While vast experimentation remains to be done in this entire field, which reveals such unlimited possibilities as applied to the study of Man and his actual nature and potentiality, enough irrefutable evidence has already been compiled to command the serious consideration and investigation of the entire scientific world.

Your opportunity for attaining this development exists now. While much remains to be discovered about mind in its operation and while many of the laws controlling the functioning of mind are yet to be known, it is nevertheless possible for you, as it has been for other earnest men and women, to greatly extend your conscious field of awareness. This elevation of your consciousness can be accomplished through the technique of meditation, the exercise of intuition, the activation of faith and the right employment of prayer.

There is profound truth in the Biblical quotation: "Seek ye first the kingdom of God and all these things shall be added unto you."

Your first step in the true development of Self should be your attunement of this Self to the God Consciousness within. Once this is done, a feeling of deep peace and inner security will take possession of you. The consciousness that is the Real You will then commence to unfold. Your personality will take on a new, more vital and more assured form of expression. Your whole tone of being and physical health will improve. The tensions and worries and discordancies of each day will begin to disappear. The ill will and resentments you have borne others will vanish. All this and more will happen to you in consciousness and be reflected in your outer world as you develop the higher sensory powers which are a part of your Great Within.

Failure to use or to attempt to use your extra sensory faculties of consciousness is limiting to the development and unfoldment of your personality. You progress in this world in exact accordance with the degree of awareness of what is going on without and within you. Any experience which enlarges this awareness, enlarges your entire horizon of activity and comprehension. When you have learned to rely to a great extent upon your intuition—God speaking to you in the form of definite feelings to do or not to do—you will make fewer mistakes and open up many otherwise unrealized opportunities in every field of endeavor. You should recognize the existence of your extra sensory perceptive powers as a natural part of your equipment, and their employment in your daily life as practical, rational and necessary.

Your five physical senses will never be outmoded but they may often be augmented and superseded by these higher powers. Once you gain reasonable control and direction of your higher senses, you can depend upon their performance at all times, with a substantial degree of accuracy. As you learn to discriminate, you will be able to accept or reject feelings that come to you in consciousness on the basis of their being right, half right or all wrong. Never limit your mind and its operation by saying that anything is impossible. Be ready to meet change with change, in life as well as in mind.

Life is actually a series of constant mental and emotional adjustments to what is happening to you and to other people. How you react may determine how they react, and how they react, in turn, often determines how you react. In fact, your emotional reaction, every waking moment of the day and night, to the experiences which come to you, determines the quality and character of the personality you are expressing.

Dare to be yourself, but be sure you *are* your *real* self. By so doing, you will so increase the appeal of your personality that you will attract right people to you, increase the love of relatives and friends for you, and acquire an inner assurance and power of expression from the God Power within which will enable you to meet every situation in life as it should be met.

To crystallize this objective in your consciousness, state this resolution with the full conviction and fervent feeling of your entire being behind it:

I recognize and accept my Personality as a gift from God, the Great Intelligence.

It is the outward expression of my Soul, my Real Self.

I know that there is no inequality in personality.

I know that my personality is my exclusive and eternal possession to develop and express as I choose.

I know that, to the degree that I can demonstrate a sincere and helpful interest in others, just to that degree does my personality become more magnetic and appealing.

To this end, I resolve to give thought each day to the fuller expression of my personality, in mind and act, by striving to overcome all feelings of fear, inferiority, self-consciousness and dislike for any person or thing.

NINE

You Have
a Special Job to Do

THOUGHT IS the only basic power in the universe. All other powers emanate from it. Intelligence is in and behind all things. When this intelligence reaches the organization of mind in Man, it becomes self-conscious. It can then be directed by the ego or identity it represents.

We know now, from what fragmentary knowledge we have been able to piece together of past ages, that creature Man, considering the short span of time he has actually been on earth, has made remarkable progress, far outdistancing any other form of life and outlasting untold millions of other species which have long since come and gone. This alone should give evidence that the consciousness which resides in Man is of a superior nature in quality to that resident in any other known life, on this planet.

Man's greatest struggle has been and still is within himself. He has seemingly conquered all other elements and forces outside himself and is in the process of causing them to do his bidding. But Man has not yet been able to understand and to harness his own thoughts and feelings.

This is the gigantic and sometimes fearsome task yet ahead of him—fearsome, because Man is dealing in his consciousness with the mightiest power in the universe. Out of his mind has come every idea which has liberated him successively from his early bondage of ignorance and superstition and has enabled him to overcome the opposition and resistance of all natural and human enemies. But some of these very ideas which have so served Man can, if his thoughts and feelings are sufficiently aroused against his fellow humans, be employed in such a manner as to destroy in a few moments' time, all he has built for himself throughout the ages.

This is the sober fact which is now causing Man primary concern. As he views the future with commingled feelings of dire misgivings and constrained hope, he has at last begun to realize that there is no material solution to the age-old problems of Man's inhumanity to man. There must be a new approach to these problems and the only approach remaining lies in the field of human consciousness itself.

It is common practice, in moments of crises, for leaders of government and religion to implore the help and guidance of God and to call upon the people for a greater exercise of faith. However well-intentioned, these beseechments are little more than hollow words touching the mere surface of human consciousness and the God Consciousness within, not at all. The only way to reach this God Consciousness is through a change in the mind and heart of the individual. The God Power cannot be flattered or coerced by any amount of praise or pleading to help Man out of his self-created dilemmas any more than God could be expected to change a tire or wash a stack of dirty dishes at the bequest of one of his creatures who might wish that such burdens and responsibilities could be taken from him.

We need to develop a rational concept of God, not as a Great Magician or Miracle Worker, but as the Father of Immutable Laws which will respond to our needs and uses only as we harmonize our thoughts and acts with them. When we do this, every prayer we utter will be answered and all the faith we exercise will be rewarded according to that faith.

Up to now, Man has sought to have God take sides against portions of His Own Creation, expecting God, in return for a professed faith in Him, to condone Man's misdeeds and help him destroy his enemies. How blind can supposedly intelligent humans be? How long can they continue to go on believing that all they need do is pray for God's help in order to receive it?

A study of history should have proved to any reasoning individual that God, as a personalized Being, does not and never has taken part in the affairs of men. If God, as so conceived, *had* taken over the affairs of the human race at any time, with the omnipotent powers imputed to Him, it is unthinkable that He would not have settled these affairs instantly and harmoniously. But to have done this would imply the necessity of cleansing the consciousness of the entire human race of all evil and destructive thoughts and feelings. It would have meant a complete elimination and cessation of God's gift of Free Will. It would have meant that God had despaired of Man's ever developing the capacity to make attunement with the God Power within and through such attunement, solve his own problems and evolve his own soul.

But such an anthropomorphic God does not exist and never did exist. Man was never meant to grovel in the dust in subjection to and worship of such a Being. He was designed to stand erect and to take his self-earned place in the scheme of creation with the aid of the God Power within him. This Power has been available to Man from the beginning in unlimited supply as he has individually learned to call upon it.

Perhaps the greatest tragedy of the ages has been the failure of religion to emphasize this very fact. Had this been done centuries ago and had Man been free to develop and spiritualize his own higher sensory faculties, he would have come to know God and to literally walk with God in his own personal life. But self-appointed religious leaders taught that God was unknowable to ordinary man and claimed that they alone were capable of communicating and interceding with God. If Man sought to worship any other concept of God apart from the church, he was condemned as a heretic or atheist and, in earlier days, was imprisoned or killed for his transgression.

Even today he is often ostracized and charged with being a disciple of Lucifer or Satan if he opposes in any way, by his views and opinions, the basic tenets of religion. It is implied that no man can possess high moral character, integrity, spiritual quality or a genuine belief in God if he is not affiliated with some church organization. For this reason, it is embarrassing to many religionists to find men and women of high character outside the church, since no one is supposed to be exemplary in thought and act without religious training. And orthodox religionists take pains to point out that such persons, regardless of their admitted goodness of character are, nevertheless, lost souls because they have not accepted the plan of salvation as offered by the church.

This attitude constitutes a world barrier against the hoped for understanding and friendly union of the peoples of the earth. Religion has not joined peoples, it has divided and segregated them.

Some world leaders are predicting that we are headed for a great religious war—that the forces of God and Anti-God are now organizing. They point to certain governments which have placed a ban on free religious worship, to the rising conflict between the followers of different faiths, to the ungodly conduct of countless humans. A few outstanding churchmen have hinted that force may be- necessary to protect and preserve Christianity.

You may even find yourself drifting into the dangerous conclusion that the only apparent way to settle differences is to have another world war and blast out of existence every country and people who appear to be opposed to your way of life.

This, of course, is no solution, as history proves—for one war, no matter how devastating, has always led to another and yet another—and always will until we, the peoples of the world, change our basic thinking. Force alone has never changed human thought.

Today it is imperative that peoples everywhere rid their minds of false and prejudiced concepts, that they learn to think for themselves, no longer restricted by geographical boundary lines and racial or religious intolerance.

Would you, if you had been born in India, have grown up a Christian?

Does not the Hindu revere his holy scripture as deeply as you do your Bible?

And the Mohammedan—and the Persian? The Egyptian? The Jew?

Is not each sincerely impelled by prejudice and hereditary affection, as natural to him as our own developed faiths are to us?

Then why should we try to win these peoples over to our faiths when we would resist being won over to theirs?

Are we not building up new and deeper resentments and hates by trying to impose our ways of thinking and belief upon others?

The growing tensions in the world today are due, in large part, to the emotionalized conflict between ideologies. No common meeting ground has been established in consciousness. These prejudiced points of difference in millions of minds are festering into surface irritations of world-wide magnitude. This is leading toward an increasing rash of outbreaks and acts of violence against the existing order of things in many countries and among many peoples.

Such will always be the tendency of humans until and unless a new accord and understanding is established in mass consciousness which eliminates age-old racial and religious antagonisms and replaces these basic animosities with the realization that Man is actually One Being divided into innumerable individualized parts, and that, as a consequence, what he does to others, he is doing to himself.

Attainment of such a vitalizing, regenerating realization is not impossible but the need for such a forward step in man's thinking toward his fellow humans must be recognized by leaders in all walks of life. Could they catch the vision and set the example, the consciousness of Man could take on cosmic dimensions overnight!

Consider, for a moment, the effect upon your own consciousness and the consciousness of all whom you, yourself, could reach—if you each could agree upon this simple statement of faith and repeat it night and morning with full acceptance and the fervent desire to make these concepts forever after a part of your life expression:

I Believe

In One God, Father of All—
In One Humanity—Every Man my Brother!
In One Common Freedom of Thought and Expression—Established Among All Races and Nations!
In One World—of Unity and Co-operation!

In One Purpose—Mutual Love and Understanding!
And in this to the End that All May Attain One Great Goal in
    Life—
Universal Peace and Happiness!

Can you see anything in this statement upon which all right thinking humans cannot agree? The Hindu, the Mohammedan, the Persian,
the Catholic, Protestant and Jew can join in such a statement of Faith
and not be in conflict with his specific religious conviction.

Lack of any great and inspired thought upon which Mankind, as a
whole, can fix its attention, in general agreement, is largely responsible
for present world discord and distrust.

If every human everywhere could daily declare, in his own native
tongue and experience in his own consciousness the same faith in Man
and in God—the universality of friendly feeling and power for good,
so engendered, would truly remake the world!

Atomic and hydrogen bombs, guided missiles, bacteriological
warfare—everything fiendish and destructive that Man can conceive
will not do it.

THOUGHT is the only power in the universe that can bring men
together or tear them apart. This fact, however, has been persistently
overlooked or disregarded. Perhaps it is because thought, in itself, is so
elusive, so unpredictable, so difficult to pin down or control. And yet,
everywhere about us, we see the evidence and result of thought, good
or bad.

It is obvious that, throughout the centuries, wrong thinking has
brought upon Man all the ills to which he is heir, and it is equally obvious that only right thinking can liberate humanity from these self-created ills. But the attempted application of any other remedial measures
never gets at the source because only thought can deal with thought.

When a man has murder in his heart, you do not remove the mur-
derous intent by confinement of the man. You only restrain, for a time,
this impulse to murder, unless you are able to reach the individual's
consciousness and release the pent-up resentments and hatreds which
have aroused the killing instinct within him.

Since Man came into being on earth, he has demonstrated an unhappy inability to get along with his fellow humans, either in the family

group or as nations. This graphically proves that life is an individual proposition and that, until you change your own thinking and attitude toward others, you cannot expect them to change theirs toward you.

United Nations may draw up plans for world peace and prosperity, debate issues loud and long with profound earnestness and sincerity, but no power or powers on earth can guarantee to you the happiness and security you desire, unless you, as an individual, do your part.

You may not feel that your little contribution to this world scene amounts to much. But you are a human, possessed of strong likes and dislikes, deep hatreds, prejudices or resentments. You have feelings and these feelings are being expressed in your daily life toward all those with whom you come in contact. It is the sum total of these feelings which you and fellow humans are expressing toward one another which has brought on this chaotic world condition.

Hitler was not alone the cause of Germany's savage conquest for world power. He was the symbol of mass feeling in Germany which demanded such a leader, at that time, and other Hitlers will rise up in the future, in other countries throughout the world, if like conditions provide provocation and opportunity. When mass feeling changes its nature, a different type and character of leader must appear to represent it.

At present, you find yourself alive in a world where the worst and the best of human elements are mixed inexorably together in a brew which gives little evidence of just what is going to boil to the top. Human thought and emotions are in great turmoil.

Ask yourself—whom do you hate? Why do you hate? What prejudices do you have? Why do you have them? Are your hates and prejudices justified? Are they based upon fact? If they are founded on fact, are you helping others or yourself by holding to these hates and prejudices? Is hating some individual or race overcoming the condition which gave rise to this hate? Is it bringing you any closer to that individual or race in understanding, tolerance or regard? If not, then your attitude, whatever the seeming justification, is wrong—and you are contributing, consciously or unconsciously, to the mounting storms of hatred and prejudice which periodically sweep over the world.

In the world of tomorrow, humans of all races and creeds are going to have to learn to live peacefully, cooperatively and happily together.

Each individual of whatever race, color or creed, should be judged in accordance with his character and his willingness to work and contribute his share to society. Our country has become the world's leading nation because of a free government which gives to a free people, comprised of all nationalities, a free opportunity to work harmoniously together for the common good. It is not until recent years that we here, have been made acutely conscious of any distinction between a Protestant, a Jew, and a Catholic.

A child recognizes no difference in the choice of his playmates of any race or denomination, unless so taught by prejudiced elders. We cannot afford to let the consciousness of our younger generation be inflamed by rabble-rousers who make a business of such excitation, or by uninformed, intolerant individuals who should know better.

"You might expect that of a Jew," a prominent man said to me, with venom in his voice.

"He's not a Jew," I said. "There's not a drop of Jewish blood in his veins."

"Well, then—he's **acting** like a Jew!" said the man, bitterly.

This is the kind of willful, blind prejudice which is doing violence to all decent attempts to better human relations.

Every race has some objectionable features. None of us is perfect. But each race, without exception, possesses many splendid qualities. Then why saddle an individual with a racial stigma?

Why not, in all fairness—*"Judge the individual—and not the race!"*

When you hold the individual of any race responsible for right conduct and accept his association on this basis, you are demanding the best of him. If you, in turn, are giving *your* best, he can give you no less without forfeiting your good will, respect and regard. No worthwhile individual will surrender such human values without putting forth a great effort in his own behalf.

But, if an individual feels himself condemned in your eyes before he has had opportunity to demonstrate his qualities of character and friendship, you are apt to bring out the worst in him.

Why shouldn't this be so? Will you go out of your way to be nice to someone who has clearly indicated that he doesn't like or trust you? The chances are that you will avoid such a person as much as possible and even say unkind things about him.

As long as you maintain and foster an intolerant attitude toward others, you are going to invite the same attitude toward you. It is an infallible law that "like attracts like."

Don't wait for the other fellow to change his thinking —change *yours!* If your thinking is wrong, you have probably passed it on to your children, wife or friends. Show them by word and deed that you hold no prejudice toward others and they will, in time, reflect your own tolerance. Look for the good things in people and appeal to this side of their natures instead of the bad.

If you begin doing this today, you will be one less person who is contributing human hate to the great ocean of consciousness. Each thinker of good thoughts helps add to the mass amount of good which eventually can exert sufficient influence to bring about better feeling and understanding between the peoples of all races and countries.

One of the coming great problems is going to revolve about the colored races, not only here but throughout the world. They have long resented, with smoldering bitterness, the brand of inferiority put upon them by the white race. These peoples are now rising to take their rightful place in the sun, striving for recognition on an equal basis with the white man.

In the United States, this problem is already economic as well as social. Education and human tolerance and understanding are needed to avert a most serious situation which, if taken out of politics and frankly and courageously met, can be solved before great damage is done.

The Negro is just as much a citizen as his white brothers and sisters, if our Constitution means what it says. He should receive equal pay in all work where he is doing the same labor as a white man or woman. If we would preserve our freedom, we must see to it that the Negro has his. He has been just as willing to serve and to die for his country. Up to now he has been largely rewarded with poor housing, unequal opportunity, and social and economic inequality.

You would not live in many of the hovels colored people are compelled to reside in. Is it any wonder there is unrest among them and a desire to invade the so- called white citizens' territory, where better homes and apartments are available?

A tremendous slum clearance program, designed to build decent, sanitary dwellings for the Negro population would accomplish wonders in improved relations between white and colored.

Give a man of any race or color a nice home, pleasant surroundings, opportunity for healthful recreation and a feeling of economic security—and you give him peace and happiness. This man will cease to covet the possessions of others or the desire to trespass. His grievances, real or imaginary, will have been relieved and he will associate harmoniously with his fellows.

The greatest example of this very fact has been life in our own country. We have been living in a land of plenty which has contained resources and room enough for our entire population. There have been opportunities for us to grow and expand. As a people we have not been hemmed in or limited in any way. We have been independent, individually, and as a nation.

But other peoples in other nations have not possessed the same boundless resources and space for expansion. They have been driven to seek relief and advancement elsewhere. Had we been placed in the same position, would we have felt impelled to fight for a better economy and social status? We must not forget that we, originally, took this land from the Indians. We took it because we wanted more individual freedom, more space, greater opportunity. And we took it without regard for the rights of the Indian who, even today, to our everlasting shame, is still denied citizenship.

Our treatment of the Indians and the Negroes is just one of the glaring inconsistencies of our American democracy which is so hard for the peoples of other countries to comprehend when we proclaim, over and over, "Freedom and Equality for all!"

The needs or wants of an average human are not excessive. They are fundamentally simple. But if we deny to others the right to earn and possess what we have gained for ourselves, we are in for trouble. Our enemies, within and without this country, are making every insidious attempt to promote discord among us, to fan our hatreds and prejudices by playing up the inequalities which still exist. The sooner we can remove these sore spots in our thinking and conduct toward segments of our own population, the more impregnable we will become against the forces that would destroy us.

Stripped of our hatreds and prejudices, we discover that we like *all* people. When men and women of varying likes and dislikes have been forced to work or fight together in a common effort for the good of all, they have forgotten their differences and have developed mutual regard and respect for one another. This will always be true because a human being is a human being, regardless of race, color or creed. Wherever he lives, he has the same basic needs of food, clothing and shelter, as well as the same love of home and country, and the same yearnings for self-betterment. These are fundamental points of similarity which never fail to unite all humans everywhere. Talk to a man of different ideological and religious convictions about experiences you both have in common and you find yourself in instant understanding and sympathy with him.

Try to change his point of view by imposing yours upon him and you arouse equally instant opposition. Man changes his point of view in life and religion and politics and all other matters through experience, not through argumentation or compulsion. The only effective appeal to any man is through feeling, not intellect. Man's reason is always swayed by *feeling*. His deep convictions based upon his life experience, if opposed to yours, will not permit him to accept your point of view, however right you may be. And you, in turn, will be just as inhibited against acceptance of his views because of your own convictions.

Judge each individual on the basis of his own character and conduct. Do not let a previous prejudice against his race or color or religion influence you. Look for the good in this man or woman. Let him see and feel that you regard him, without reservation, as a fellow human. Place upon him the responsibility of living up to your estimate of him.

It is an axiom of life that you get just what you give out. Each individual has something no other person possesses to give to the world. You can help him give it by maintaining the right attitude toward him and he, in turn, can help you render greater service by co-operation and fellowship with you.

You will never understand the other fellow so long as you hold aloof and refuse to have anything to do with him. Only through association for the common good is real understanding between humans of all nationalities and faiths achieved.

It will not be easy, at first, to remove false and prejudiced concepts from consciousness since many of them have become so deep-seated through the years.

As a start, give your full and conscientious attention to the statement of Faith contained in this chapter. Repeat it, thoughtfully and feelingly, over and over. Let it permeate your consciousness until it has enlarged your mental horizons to take in all humanity

Meditate upon this statement and all that its realization can mean to Mankind. Such meditation will raise the level of your thoughts and bring attunement with the God Consciousness within.

And remember, the world about you can never change until you, as an individual, change.

No one exactly like you in form or personality expression has ever been born in all the aeons of time which have preceded this moment, and no one precisely resembling you will ever be born in all the aeons of time yet to come. God, the Father-Mother of this universe has created and is creating no duplicates. You may have considered yourself small and insignificant in the sight of God, even in the sight of man, but you, basically, are not. No one is equipped to do quite the job you can do on this earth, once you find your real self and purpose in life and learn how to develop and express your personality as God, the Great Intelligence intended.

It is my conviction, based on a lifetime study and personal reflection, as I have emphasized, that you are an individualized, segmentized part of God, the Great Intelligence, in process of developing your soul through the manner in which you react to the experiences you are having here. This means that everything you think and do does count. The more you can develop your mind and soul and personality, the more prepared you will be to enter into the great experiences which are coming toward you in time.

All humans are destined to discover that human life has a far greater cosmic value than they have ever yet sensed or imagined. The realization will then come that all the ills of this world are man-made, that God, the Great Intelligence is in His Heaven, and that all is fundamentally right with the universe. Only we are wrong because we have been, thus far, out of attunement with and unaware of the God Presence within. Once this attunement has been realized by a sufficient number of humans, the peace that has been long sought and never achieved between peoples, will come to pass on this earth.

This great goal starts—with YOU.

THE END

Made in the USA
Middletown, DE
13 February 2024

49697287R00087